LOW-FODMAP
DIET COOKBOOK

Overcoming Irritable Bowel Syndrome with Nourishing,
Delightful, And Healing recipes and
a Comprehensive Guide to Understanding
and Treating Your Symptoms

Robert K. Edwards

Copyright 2023© Robert K. Edwards

IMPORTANT, READ CAREFULLY: MEDICAL DISCLAIMER

This book is provided for educational and informational purposes only and does not constitute the provision of medical advice. The information provided should not be used to diagnose or treat any health problem or disease, and individuals seeking personal medical advice should consult a licensed physician.

Always seek the advice of your doctor or another qualified healthcare professional regarding any medical condition. Never ignore professional medical advice or delay seeking it because of something you have read in this book. Before using the food recipes in this book, it is advisable to consult a physician to ensure they are appropriate for your personal physical condition.

INTRODUCTION

Diets that are low in fermentable oligosaccharides, polyols, and polyol esters (Low-FODMAP diets) are one strategy for treating digestive issues, in particular irritable bowel syndrome (IBS) and other digestive problems. Fermentable Oligosaccharides, Disaccharides, Monosaccharides, and Polyols are what are referred to when using the acronym FODMAP. These are the kinds of carbohydrates that can be difficult to digest for some individuals, causing them to experience symptoms such as bloating, gas, and abdominal pain.

The Low-FODMAP diet is intended to reduce the consumption of these types of carbohydrates, which, for some people, can alleviate the discomfort associated with digestive symptoms. The diet requires that certain foods that are high in FODMAPs be avoided or limited, and that these foods be replaced with alternatives that are low in FODMAPs. The objective is to determine which foods bring on symptoms and which foods are tolerated well so that an individualised strategy for a diet that will be followed over the long term can be developed.

In recent years, this approach to managing digestive symptoms has gained popularity as a result of the increased amount of research that has been conducted on the link between diet and the health of the digestive tract. Following a low-FODMAP diet has helped a lot of people find relief from their symptoms, and there are now a lot of resources available to help people figure out how to properly follow the diet.

One of these resources is a cookbook called the Low-FODMAP Diet Cookbook. This cookbook offers a collection of recipes that are designed to be low in FODMAPs while still being tasty and satisfying. A variety of recipes for breakfast, lunch, and dinner are included in the cookbook, in addition to suggestions for organising meals and going grocery shopping.

In addition to the recipes, the Low-FODMAP Diet Cookbook provides an overview of the diet as well as the research that supports it. This book discusses a variety of topics related to digestive health, including the function of FODMAPs, the symptoms of irritable bowel syndrome and other digestive disorders, and the ways in which a low-FODMAP diet can assist in the management of these symptoms.

DIET

What are fodmap food?

Short-chain carbohydrates are what make up FODMAPs. These carbohydrates are poorly absorbed by the body. Fermentable Oligosaccharides, Disaccharides, Monosaccharides, and Polyols is what the acronym stands for. Carbohydrates like these can be found in a wide variation of foods and drinks, like fruits, vegetables, grains, and dairy products, among others. People who suffer from digestive disorders such as irritable bowel syndrome may experience gastrointestinal distress as a result of eating foods high in fermentable oligosaccharides, polyols, and monosaccharides (FODMAPs) (IBS).

It is possible that a diet low in FODMAPs will be recommended for the management of these symptoms. This method entails avoiding foods high in FODMAPs for a set amount of time, usually between two and six weeks, and then gradually reintroducing them in order to determine which ones are responsible for triggering symptoms.

Foods that are high in FODMAP include:

Oligosaccharides are a type of sugar that can be found in a variety of foods, including wheat, rye, onions, garlic, and legumes.

Disaccharides are a type of carbohydrate that can be found in dairy products like milk, yoghurt, and soft cheeses.

Monosaccharides are a type of sugar that can be found in honey and a variety of fruits, including apples, mangoes, and watermelon.

Polyols are a type of sugar alcohol that can be found naturally in certain fruits like blackberries, cherries, and nectarines as well as in some artificial sweeteners like sorbitol and xylitol.

Vegetables such as carrots, cucumbers, tomatoes, zucchini, and bell peppers are examples of foods that are low in FODMAPs.

Fruits including bananas, blueberries, grapes, oranges, and strawberries are examples of fruits. Grains include things like oats, quinoa, rice, and gluten-free versions of things like bread and pasta.

alternatives to dairy products such as lactose-free yoghurt and almond milk are available.

It is essential to keep in mind that a diet low in FODMAPs should not be followed for an extended period of time since doing so might result in nutritional deficits. It is recommended that this procedure be carried out only under the supervision of a licenced dietician or another appropriately trained healthcare practitioner.

Hence, FODMAPs are short-chain carbohydrates that are present in a wide variety of meals and beverages. Those who suffer from digestive diseases are more likely to experience pain as a result of their consumption of certain foods, even if they may not be harmful to everyone. It is possible that a diet low in FODMAPs may be prescribed to help manage these symptoms; however, following such a diet should only be done so under the supervision of an appropriately trained medical expert.

Causes of inflammation of the gut

The digestive system is a complex organ that plays a significant role in maintaining both our individual well-being and our overall physical health. It is responsible for the digesting process, the absorption of nutrients, and the elimination of waste products from the body. Nevertheless, inflammation in the stomach may result in a number of unpleasant symptoms, such as cramping in the abdominal region, diarrhea, and bloating. These symptoms may have been brought on by a variety of underlying conditions. In certain people, Crohn's disease and ulcerative colitis may develop from chronic inflammation of the gastrointestinal system, which has been related to the development of more serious disorders. In this article, we will talk about some of the more common reasons that may contribute to inflammation in the gastrointestinal system, as well as some of the possible treatments for that inflammation.

Inflammation in the gastrointestinal system may be caused by a number of factors, one of the most important of which is an imbalance in the microbiome of the gut. The digestive system is home to billions of different species of microorganisms, including bacteria, viruses, and other kinds of microbes. Together, these microbes make up the microbiome of the gut. When this precarious equilibrium is thrown off, it may lead to either an increase in potentially harmful bacteria or a decrease in bacteria that are beneficial to the environment. Both of these eventualities are to be avoided at all costs. Because of this imbalance, the immune system in the stomach may have a response, which may subsequently lead to inflammation. The use of antibiotics, which may wreak havoc on the microbiota of the gut, is a common cause of inflammation in the digestive system. This inflammation can lead to a number of health complications.

Another key factor that contributes to inflammation in the digestive system is a diet that is high in processed foods and sweets that have been refined. It has been shown that some types of meals promote the growth of harmful bacteria in the stomach, which may result in inflammation. This may be a contributing factor in several inflammatory conditions. On the other side, consuming a diet that is rich in whole foods, like fruits, vegetables, and grains that have not been processed, may help to reduce inflammation and provide nourishment for the beneficial bacteria that are located in the digestive tract.

The inflammation that might develop in the digestive system may be exacerbated by stress, which is another another factor that may be involved. When we are put under a lot of stress, it has the ability to trigger the body's stress response, which in turn has the potential to induce inflammation in a variety of different parts of the body, including the digestive system. This may be a problem when we are trying to lose weight. Stress that lasts for an extended period of time may also disrupt the delicate balance of the microbiome in the stomach, which may ultimately lead to inflammation.

Inflammation of the gastrointestinal tract may be brought on not only by the impact that these factors have, but also by the use of certain medications. It has been shown that nonsteroidal anti-inflammatory drugs (NSAIDs) such as aspirin and ibuprofen, amongst others, irritate the lining of the stomach, which may ultimately lead to inflammation of the stomach lining. In a similar fashion, the use of chemotherapy drugs may cause inflammation of the gastrointestinal system as a side effect. This can occur in both adults and children.

Intestinal intolerances and food allergies are two more common factors that contribute to inflammation in the digestive system. If the body is unable to efficiently digest certain types of food, it may set off an immunological response in the stomach, which in turn may lead to inflammation. This reaction may also cause the stomach to become irritated. There are many different kinds of food intolerances, but two of the most prevalent are lactose intolerance and gluten intolerance. It is possible that persons who are allergic to specific foods may also have inflammation in their digestive system.

Inflammation that has been present in other parts of the body for an extended period of time may also produce inflammation in the stomach. This is the last and most important point. For instance, inflammation that is chronic in the joints, such as that which is observed in rheumatoid arthritis, may lead to inflammation that is chronic in the stomach. This is because the joints and the stomach are both made up of connective tissue. Psoriasis is an example of a disorder that produces chronic inflammation in the skin, which may also contribute to inflammation in the gut. Inflammation in the gut may also be caused by psoriasis.

An imbalance in the gut flora, a diet high in processed foods, stress, certain drugs, food intolerances and allergies, and chronic inflammation in other parts of the body can all be potential contributors to inflammation of the gut. Inflammation of the gut can also be caused by allergic reactions to certain foods. If the underlying reasons of this inflammation are recognized and handled in the proper way, it is possible to reduce inflammation in the gut and improve overall gut health. This may be accomplished by increasing the overall health of the gut.

Symptoms of inflammation

Inflammation is the body's natural defense mechanism, and it occurs whenever the immune system identifies a potential danger, such as a wound, an infection, or an irritant. Symptoms of this illness include redness, swelling, warmth, and discomfort in the affected location, and possibly a loss of function in that area. When it comes to defining the symptoms that are brought on by inflammation, the severity of the condition, as well as the location of the affected body part, plays a significant impact.

One of the symptoms of inflammation that people feel the most often is pain. Pain might be described as a smoldering sensation, a quick stabbing agony, or even as a gradual aching. These are just some of the many ways that pain can manifest itself. It is also conceivable for it to remain isolated, but depending on the place that is inflamed, it may be broad. Another possibility is that it will not spread. Inflammation may also be the source of discomfort or sensitivity to touch in the area that is currently being affected by the condition.

An other characteristic indication of inflammation is swelling in the region that is afflicted. The accumulation of fluid leads to swelling, which is produced by increased blood flow to the affected area, which in turn leads to an increase in blood flow. This cycle continues until the affected region is completely swollen. Depending on the extent of the swelling and whether or not it is widespread, the area that is affected may have a feeling of being restricted or constricted.

The manifestation of redness is yet another distinctive symptom that inflammation is present. It occurs when there is an increase in the blood flow to the affected location, which causes the area to appear red or pink. This condition is known as a hematoma. A hematoma is the medical term for this situation. A sense of warmth or heat in the region that is affected, which may occur in combination with redness in the area, is another characteristic indicator of inflammation. Inflammation may cause the area to become red.

In certain cases, one of the indications of inflammation is a high fever, which may also be present in the affected individual in question. Fever is the term used to describe the condition that occurs when the internal temperature of the body rises over the usual range. The onset of fever is often precipitated by a disease or inflammation. When a person has a fever, it is not unusual for them to also exhibit other symptoms, such as shivering, sweating, and feeling exhausted.

There is a possibility that inflammation might result in a loss of function in the area that is being impacted. This occurs when the inflammation disrupts the normally occurring functions of the area that is being affected by it. Inflammation in the joints, for instance, may lead to stiffness and a reduction in mobility, while inflammation in the lungs can lead to difficulty breathing. Inflammation may be the root cause of one or both of these symptoms.

In unusual cases, inflammation may also be the cause of other symptoms, such as weariness, headaches, and stiffness in the muscles. This is a rare possibility, though. In the vast majority of instances, the underlying sickness that is creating the inflammation (as opposed to the inflammation itself) is accountable for these symptoms, rather than the inflammation itself being the cause of these symptoms.

Inflammation is the body's natural defense mechanism, and it occurs whenever the immune system identifies a potential danger, such as a wound, an infection, or an irritant. When it comes to defining the symptoms that are brought on by inflammation, the severity of the condition, as well as the location of the affected body part, plays a significant impact. Pain, swelling, redness, warmth, and a loss of function in the area that is affected are the most typical symptoms of inflammation. Inflammation is characterized by a range of symptoms, the most frequent of which are listed above. If you have any of these symptoms, it is very important that you get medical attention as soon as you possibly can. This will allow the underlying cause of the inflammation to be determined, and you will be able to obtain the appropriate treatment.

Types of inflammation

In order for this intricate process to be carried out, it is necessary for a large number of cells and chemicals located throughout the body to become active. There are several diverse types of inflammation, each of which is defined in a unique way and is brought on by a different collection of contributing variables.

Acute inflammation is the most common kind of inflammation and affects almost everyone at some point. It is a rapid response that does not continue for a very long time and it takes occur within minutes or hours after an accident or disease has taken place. Acute inflammation may be identified by its distinctive symptoms, which include redness, swelling, heat, pain, and loss of function. If any of these symptoms are present, then acute inflammation is present. This is a controlled reaction, and the end objective is to eliminate the hazardous material while maintaining its confined space.

On the other hand, chronic inflammation is a prolonged and persistent response that may last for weeks, months, or even years at a time. Chronic inflammation can be caused by a number of different factors. Inflammation of this kind may be brought on by a variety of different underlying conditions. A number of degenerative illnesses, including arthritis, asthma, diabetes, and heart disease, have been related to inflammation that lasts for an extended period of time. It is a systemic response, which means that it involves the whole body, and it has the potential to lead to damage in the tissues as well as dysfunction in those tissues. Furthermore, it involves the entire body.

Granulomatous inflammation is a type of chronic inflammation that is characterized by the formation of granulomas, which are small clusters of immune cells that surround and isolate foreign bodies such as bacteria, fungi, or foreign particles. Granulomas are formed when there is an overabundance of neutrophils, which are white blood cells that are responsible for fighting infection. Granulomas are formed when there is an excessive number of neutrophils in the blood. Neutrophils are white blood cells that are responsible for warding off infections. Granulomatous inflammation is a defensive reaction that seeks to limit the spread of infectious pathogens. However, if it is allowed to continue, it may also lead to damage to the tissue and scarring.

A type of inflammation known as autoimmune inflammation takes place when the immune system of the body mistakenly attacks healthy tissues and organs located within the body. Inflammation can take many forms, including autoimmune inflammation. Rheumatoid arthritis, multiple sclerosis, and lupus are just few of the autoimmune diseases that may be traced back to inflammation brought on by the body's own immune system. It is a response that lasts for a long time and spreads throughout the body, and it has the ability to have an influence on a variety of organs and systems inside the body.

An allergic response to an allergen, such as pollen, dust, or animal dander, may produce inflammation of the immune system. This kind of inflammation is referred to as allergic inflammation. An allergic reaction is a localized response that involves the activation of immune cells such as eosinophils and mast cells. Allergies may be caused by a number of different substances. Because of this, an allergic irritation will develop. It is the culprit behind allergy symptoms such as hives, sneezing, and itching in the affected area. Avoiding the allergen is the best way to stop yourself from getting allergic reactions.

Infectious inflammation is a kind of inflammation that manifests itself as a response to infectious organisms like bacteria, viruses, or parasites. Inflammation may take many forms. Infectious inflammation is a rapid and systemic reaction that involves the activation of a wide variety of immune cells and chemicals to fight off the infection. We are going to eliminate the infectious agent, and we are also going to prevent it from spreading to other parts of the body. Inflammation is the general term used to describe the response of the body to harmful stimuli such as cuts, infections, or any number of other potentially harmful stimuli. The process of inflammation consists of many different stages and is constantly evolving. There are several diverse types of inflammation, each of which is defined in a unique way and is brought on by a different collection of contributing variables. If you have a firm grasp of the many different types of inflammation, it may be of great aid when it comes to the diagnosis, treatment, and prevention of a broad variety of diseases and conditions.

Health risks

The body's normal reaction to a wound or an infection is inflammation; nevertheless, inflammation that lasts for an extended period of time may have detrimental effects on one's health. According to the findings of several studies, chronic inflammation may have a role in the progression of a wide variety of illnesses, including cancer, diabetes, and cardiovascular disease.

Chronic inflammation is connected with a number of significant health hazards, one of the most significant of which is an increased risk of cardiovascular disease. Inflammation may cause damage to the blood arteries, which can lead to the production of plaques. Plaques can obstruct blood flow, which can raise the chance of having a heart attack or a stroke. Inflammation has also been proven to have a role in the development of various cardiovascular disorders, such as atherosclerosis and peripheral artery disease, according to research done on the subject.

Inflammation is associated with an increased risk of diabetes, which is another potential health issue. Insulin resistance may be caused by chronic inflammation, which can ultimately result in high blood sugar levels and the development of type 2 diabetes. Persistent inflammation can also cause tissue damage. Inflammation has been shown to have a role in the development of various metabolic illnesses, such as metabolic syndrome and obesity.

Chronic inflammation has been associated to an increased risk of many different forms of cancer, in addition to its association with diabetes and cardiovascular disease. Damage to DNA and mutations caused by it may both be caused by inflammation, which can play a role in the development of cancer. Many forms of cancer, including lung cancer, colon cancer, and breast cancer, have been proven to be associated with chronic inflammation, which may raise the chance of developing these cancers.

Inflammation has also been linked to a wide variety of other health problems, some of which are autoimmune diseases like lupus and rheumatoid arthritis. Under these circumstances, the immune system of the body will mistakenly attack healthy cells, which will result in inflammation and damage to the tissues.

Inflammation that is chronic may also play a role in the development of mental health issues such as anxiety and depression. There is a connection between inflammation and alterations in the chemistry of the brain, which can result in symptoms such as tiredness, irritability, and difficulty concentrating.

There are various variables that might lead to chronic inflammation, including poor nutrition, lack of exercise, and stress. Inflammation may be caused by eating a diet that is heavy in processed foods and saturated fats; on the other hand, eating a diet that is high in fruits, vegetables, and healthy fats can help decrease inflammation. A reduction in inflammation may also be achieved by the use of stress management strategies like meditation and yoga, in addition to physical activity.

An increased risk of cardiovascular disease, diabetes, cancer, and other health issues may be one of the major health repercussions that can result from chronic inflammation. It is essential to take measures to minimize inflammation, such as switching to a nutritious diet, being more physically active on a regular basis, and learning to better manage stress. We can help minimize our chance of getting these significant health conditions and increase general health and wellbeing by acting in this way.

Low-Fodmap Diet

In recent years, low-FODMAP diets have been more popular, particularly among those who suffer from irritable bowel syndrome (IBS). These diets restrict foods that are rich in fermentable oligosaccharides, disulfides, monosaccharides, and polyols (FODMAP) (IBS). The group of carbohydrates known as FODMAPs have been given its own category. The small intestine has a difficult time absorbing these carbs, which may lead to gastrointestinal distress in the form of bloating, gas, and stomach pain. It has been shown that the low-FODMAP diet, which limits the consumption of carbohydrates that fall into particular categories, is an effective treatment for irritable bowel syndrome (IBS) in many people.

In order to adhere to the guidelines of the low-FODMAP diet, some food groups must be severely limited or totally avoided. These include foods that are high in lactose content, such as dairy products and items based on wheat, in addition to certain fruits and vegetables, such as apples and pears, onions, and garlic. Those who are sensitive to FODMAPs may feel stomach pain as a consequence of the high FODMAP content of particular meals. This is because FODMAPs are carbohydrates that are poorly absorbed by the gut. In most cases, the diet will start with a period known as "elimination," during which the aforementioned items will be removed from the diet entirely for a certain length of time. After this, there will be a period of reintroduction, during which these foods will be progressively reintroduced in order to discover which foods can be ingested safely. This will take place in order to find out which foods may be consumed safely.

Although the low-FODMAP diet has been demonstrated to be an effective treatment for irritable bowel syndrome (IBS), it is essential to keep in mind that it is a restricted diet, which may be challenging to maintain for an extended period of time. This is something that must be kept in mind at all times. It is likely that some individuals may find that the diet needs be modified in order for it to meet their specific requirements. If this occurs, the diet will need to be adjusted accordingly. For instance, some individuals may find that they are able to tolerate specific foods even though they contain FODMAPs in little amounts, whereas other people may find that they are needed to completely avoid particular things.

One of the probable negatives of the low-FODMAP diet is that there is a chance that the diet may not include enough of certain nutrients, such as fiber and calcium. This is a possibility. This is because many foods that are high in fiber, such as legumes and some fruits and vegetables, also tend to be high in FODMAPs. Some examples of these kinds of foods include: Those who follow the low-FODMAP diet may need extra nutritional assistance in the form of supplements or the exploration of other sources of these components in order to maintain optimal health.

It is also extremely important to note that the low-FODMAP diet is not the optimal choice for everyone. This is something that should not be overlooked. In order to maintain their health, people who have certain disorders, such as celiac disease, may be necessary to make adjustments to the foods and beverages that they consume on a regular basis. Also, before commencing the low-FODMAP diet, it is vital to obtain the counsel of a skilled medical practitioner in order to ensure that the diet is appropriate for you. This is due to the fact that the diet has the potential to create undesirable consequences, and it may not be appropriate for those who have certain medical issues, as well as for women who are pregnant or nursing. Individuals who have irritable bowel syndrome (IBS) could discover that following a diet low in fermentable carbohydrates, oligosaccharides, and polyols (low-FODMAP) is an effective therapy choice for their condition. It is a pretty simple procedure that does not need any type of invasive therapy, and it has the potential to be useful in a wide variety of different circumstances. In addition to this, it acts as a strong basis for constructing a specific diet plan and evaluating which meals may function as probable triggers. In other words, it helps you avoid food triggers.

The low-FODMAP diet is a kind of eating plan that involves limiting the consumption of certain types of carbohydrates in order to alleviate the symptoms of irritable bowel syndrome (IBS). These symptoms might include abdominal pain, bloating, gas, and diarrhea. It is essential to emphasize that this is a calorie- and macronutrient-restricted diet, which may be difficult to follow for an extended period of time and may also be deficient in some nutrients. In spite of the fact that it may be effective, it is quite important to bear in mind that this diet. Before beginning the diet, it is important to have a conversation about your medical history with a trained medical professional and work together with a registered dietitian to create a personalized meal plan that takes into account all of your particular dietary requirements. Only then should you start the diet.

Benefits of a low-fodmap diet

Those who suffer with irritable bowel syndrome may find relief from their symptoms by following a diet known as a low-FODMAP diet, which is a sort of elimination diet (IBS). This diet eliminates certain kinds of carbohydrates known as FODMAPs (fermentable oligosaccharides, disaccharides, monosaccharides, and polyols). These types of carbohydrates are poorly absorbed in the small intestine and are known to cause gastrointestinal symptoms such as bloating, gas, and diarrhea.

The efficacy of a low-FODMAP diet in relieving symptoms of irritable bowel syndrome (IBS) is one of the most significant advantages of following such a diet. Studies have indicated that persons with IBS who eat a diet that is low in fructooligosaccharides (FODMAPs) enjoy a substantial reduction in the severity of their symptoms. Due to the fact that persons with IBS often experience pain, humiliation, and social isolation as a consequence of their symptoms, this has the potential to result in a higher quality of life.

A diet low in fructooligosaccharides, oligosaccharides, and polyols (low-FODMAP diet) may improve symptoms of irritable bowel syndrome (IBS) For instance, it could lower inflammation in the stomach, which would be beneficial to the general health of the gut. In addition, there is evidence from some studies that following a diet low in fructose, oligofructose, and lactose (low-FODMAP) may help people who suffer from other digestive disorders, such as inflammatory bowel disease (IBD).

One further advantage of following a low-FODMAP diet is that it is adaptable to the specific requirements of each person. People can figure out which specific FODMAPs bring on their symptoms by following this diet's two-step process, which begins with a period of elimination and is followed by a phase of reintroduction. This indicates that individuals are able to create a personalized diet that allows them to enjoy as many foods as possible while avoiding only the FODMAPs that cause symptoms in their condition.

In spite of the fact that it has a number of positive aspects, adhering to a low-FODMAP diet can be difficult because it necessitates making significant adjustments to one's usual patterns of food consumption. The elimination phase can be especially challenging for people because it requires them to abstain from eating a wide variety of commonly consumed foods that contain high levels of FODMAPs. Because of this, individuals may find it difficult to find appropriate foods when dining out or participating in social events, which can result in feelings of frustration, boredom, and social isolation.

It is essential to keep in mind that adhering to a low-FODMAP diet is something that should only be done so under the supervision of an appropriately trained medical expert, such as a registered dietitian. This is due to the fact that the diet may be somewhat restricted in terms of nutrition, and as a result, some individuals may unwittingly leave out vital elements from their diet. Those who follow a low-FODMAP diet may benefit from the assistance of a dietician, who can not only verify that they are receiving all of the necessary nutrients but also provide support and direction all the way through the elimination and reintroduction stages.

A diet that is low in fructooligosaccharides, oligosaccharides, monosaccharides, and polyols (low-FODMAP diet) has shown promise as a successful treatment for irritable It is a personalized diet that enables individuals to determine the particular FODMAPs that bring on their symptoms and steer clear of those foods. Nonetheless, it is essential to begin this diet under the direction of a qualified medical practitioner, since it may be difficult to stick to and may be limiting in terms of nutrition if it is not well handled. Those who suffer from irritable bowel syndrome (IBS) and other digestive diseases may find considerable relief by following a diet low in fermentable carbohydrates, yeast, garlic, and onion (low-FODMAP).

Foods to avoid

While though inflammation is a necessary part of the healing process, there is still a possibility that it can become chronic and lead to persistent health issues if it is not properly managed. One strategy that may be used in the fight against chronic inflammation is the consumption of a nourishing diet. It is well established that some meals may make inflammation worse, while other foods have been shown to have the opposite effect. In this piece, we will discuss the foods that you need to stay away from eating if you want to lessen the effects of inflammation or prevent it from happening in the first place.

Foods That Have Undergone Some Kind Of Processing There is a high probability that processed foods will be high in levels of sugar, trans fats, and additives. They often have a low nutrient density but a high calorie count due to their heavy consumption. Consuming processed foods may lead to chronic inflammation, as shown by a number of studies. This, in turn, might increase one's risk for a range of illnesses and disorders, such as cardiovascular disease, diabetes, and cancer. Some examples of processed foods are drinks with added sugar, snack foods, and ready-to-eat meals that have already been prepackaged.

Carbohydrates That Have Been Undergone a Process of Refining The fiber level of refined carbohydrates is modest, while the sugar amount may be rather high. You may find them in a variety of foods, including white bread, spaghetti, and other baked goods, among other locations. Consuming refined carbohydrates may, as shown by a number of studies, result in an increase in systemic inflammation throughout the body. Instead, it is best to go for meals that are prepared with whole grains, such as quinoa, brown rice, and bread that is made with whole wheat flour.

As a result of the frying process, most fried foods have a high calorie and fat content that is not good for you. They are often cooked in oils that have a high concentration of omega-6 fatty acids, which, if ingested in sufficient amounts, may induce inflammation everywhere throughout the body. This may be avoided by cooking them in oils that do not contain omega-6 fatty acids. Donuts, fried chicken, and french fries are a few examples of foods and snacks that are prepared via frying. Rather than that, it is recommended that you choose foods that have been cooked by grilling, baking, or broiling the INGREDIENTS.

Both red and processed meat are high in the saturated fats that may contribute to inflammation throughout the body. Saturated fats are found in meat. Red and processed meats both contain high levels of saturated fats. They also include a high quantity of advanced glycation end products, which are more often referred to as AGEs. These advanced glycation end products have been associated to inflammation as well as oxidative stress. Red and processed meats such as beef, bacon, and sausage are all examples of this kind of meat. Ham is another another illustration of this. Tofu, fish, and chicken are all examples of lean proteins that are better alternatives to red meat since they contain less fat.

Products Derived from Milk and Other Animals Used for Producing Dairy Saturated fats, which are found in high concentration in dairy products, are a potential contributor to inflammation throughout the body. Casein is one of the proteins that can be found in them, and it is the kind of protein that has the potential to provoke an inflammatory response as well as a response from the immune system. Dairy goods include things like milk, cheese, and butter, among other things. Among the several dairy products is yogurt. It is recommended that one avoid typical dairy products in favor of non-dairy alternatives such as almond milk, coconut milk, and vegan cheese. Other non-dairy alternatives include

Drinking an excessive quantity of alcohol has been shown to increase the risk of inflammation throughout the body. This impact is most pronounced when a big quantity of alcohol is consumed at once. In addition, it is possible that it will cause damage to the liver in addition to contributing to other health problems. It is recommended that women limit their alcohol consumption to no more than one drink per day, while men should limit themselves to no more than two drinks per day.

Plant-Based Oils or Plant-Derived Oils Canola oil, soybean oil, and maize oil are all examples of vegetable oils that contain a substantial quantity of omega-6 fatty acids, which are known to contribute to inflammation throughout the body. Soybean oil also contains omega-6 fatty acids. Instead, you should think about choosing healthy fats such as olive oil, avocado oil, and coconut oil. These are just a few examples. This is the suggestion that has been made.

Inflammation is a natural process that takes place within the body; however, inflammation that lasts for an extended period of time may be associated with a number of different health problems. It is possible to reduce the amount of inflammation that is present in the body by reducing the amount of processed foods, refined carbohydrates, fried foods, red and processed meats, dairy products, alcoholic drinks, and vegetable oils that are consumed. In addition to keeping an overall balanced diet, choosing meals that are rich in whole grains, lean proteins, alternatives to dairy products, and healthy fats is an excellent way to achieve a healthy body and avoid chronic inflammation.

Foods that are suitable with moderation

Foods that are suitable with moderation in regards to low FODMAP diet can be challenging to identify. A low FODMAP diet is a dietary approach that involves restricting foods that are high in FODMAPs - fermentable oligosaccharides, disaccharides, monosaccharides, and polyols. These types of carbohydrates are poorly absorbed in the small intestine, which can lead to bloating, gas, abdominal pain, and other digestive symptoms in people with irritable bowel syndrome (IBS) or other digestive disorders.

If you're following a low FODMAP diet, it's essential to know which foods you can eat in moderation. Here are some examples:

Dairy products: Dairy products such as milk, cheese, and yogurt can be high in lactose, which is a type of FODMAP. However, some people with IBS can tolerate small amounts of lactose. Hard cheeses, such as cheddar and Parmesan, are typically lower in lactose than soft cheeses.

Fruits: Most fruits are high in FODMAPs, but some are suitable for a low FODMAP diet in moderation. These include bananas, blueberries, grapes, kiwi fruit, mandarins, oranges, and strawberries. It's important to note that the serving size matters, and it's best to avoid eating large amounts of fruit in one sitting.

Vegetables: Vegetables are an essential part of a healthy diet, but some are high in FODMAPs. Moderation is key when it comes to low FODMAP vegetables. Examples of suitable vegetables include broccoli, carrot, eggplant, green beans, kale, lettuce, tomato, and zucchini.

Grains: Grains such as wheat, rye, and barley are high in FODMAPs and should be avoided on a low FODMAP diet. However, some grains are suitable in moderation, such as oats, quinoa, and rice. It's important to choose whole grain options and avoid processed grains that contain high FODMAP INGREDIENTS.

Proteins: Most proteins, such as meat, poultry, fish, and eggs, are low in FODMAPs and suitable for a low FODMAP diet. However, some protein sources, such as legumes, soy products, and some nuts, are high in FODMAPs and should be consumed in moderation.

Fats and oils: Fats and oils are low in FODMAPs and suitable for a low FODMAP diet. However, it's important to choose healthy fats, such as olive oil, avocado oil, and nuts, and avoid processed oils that may contain high FODMAP INGREDIENTS.

Sweeteners: Many sweeteners, such as honey, high fructose corn syrup, and agave, are high in FODMAPs and should be avoided on a low FODMAP diet. However, some sweeteners, such as stevia and glucose, are low in FODMAPs and suitable in moderation.

Following a low FODMAP diet can be challenging, but with the right knowledge and guidance, it is possible to identify suitable foods that can be eaten in moderation. It's important to work with a healthcare professional or a registered dietitian to create a personalized low FODMAP diet plan that meets your nutritional needs and helps manage your digestive symptoms.

The importance of exercise and a healthy lifestyle

Eating properly, being active on a regular basis, and avoiding smoking are three of the most important things that we can do to improve our overall health. Leading a healthy lifestyle is one of the most important things that we can do. Regular physical activity is one of the most essential components of a healthy lifestyle, and it should be a priority for everyone. Regular exercise has been shown to have a broad variety of beneficial impacts on both our physical and mental health. These benefits include reducing the risk of acquiring chronic disorders such as diabetes and heart disease, as well as improving our mood and our ability to think clearly. The control of inflammation is one of the most essential components of a healthy lifestyle, alongside physical exercise, which is one of the most important components of a healthy living. While inflammation is a normal process that happens in the body in response to injury or infection, chronic inflammation may lead to a range of health concerns, including arthritis, cardiovascular disease, and cancer. The body goes through a process known as inflammation in reaction to a noxious stimulus like an injury or an illness. We are in luck since there are a lot of things that we can do to decrease the impacts of inflammation and to develop a healthy physique inside ourselves.

Consuming a diet rich in nutrients is one of the most effective ways to lower inflammation levels in the body down to a more manageable level. Consuming foods that are high in antioxidants, such as fruits, vegetables, and grains that are whole, may be able to help the body in its fight against the free radicals that are the root cause of inflammation. Some meals are a potential source of these free radicals in the body. In addition, it may be beneficial to reduce inflammation in the body by avoiding processed meals, sweets, and consuming excessive quantities of alcohol.

Stress is an additional factor that has been hypothesized to have a part in the pathogenesis of inflammation. When we are under stress, our bodies create a hormone called cortisol, which has been linked to the beginning of inflammatory reactions. When we are under stress, our bodies produce more of this hormone. It is vital, in order to bring down the degree of inflammation that is present in the body, to discover ways of stress management such as the practice of meditation, yoga, or deep breathing exercises.

In addition, getting a enough quantity of sleep is very necessary for bringing inflammation levels down. A lack of sleep may cause disruptions in the natural processes that occur in our body, and it can also play a role in the development of chronic inflammation. In order to facilitate the formation of healthy sleeping habits, it is important to ensure that you get between seven and eight hours of sleep each night and to establish a regular sleep regimen.

The regular performance of physical activity is yet another critical component in the battle against inflammation. In addition to enhancing one's overall fitness and health, engaging in consistent physical activity may also assist to reduce the amount of inflammation that is already present in the body. It is recommended that exercises of a moderate intensity be undertaken on most days of the week, such as brisk walking or cycling, with the objective of clocking at least half an hour every day.

In addition to engaging in regular physical exercise, including other healthy habits into your daily routine, such as maintaining a balanced diet and obtaining an adequate amount of sleep, may also help to reduce inflammation. For instance, giving up smoking, reducing one's use of alcohol, and maintaining a healthy weight are all things that may help to develop a healthier body and reduce inflammation. Keeping one's weight at a reasonable level is also important.

Regular physical activity is a vital component of having a healthy lifestyle, and there are many different ways in which it may be of assistance to us as individuals. Doing regular exercise may help improve our mental health and mood, as well as our cardiovascular health, immune system, strength, and flexibility. This is in addition to the other health benefits associated with exercise. Also, it has the potential to help strengthen our immune system. In maintaining a regular exercise routine, one may reduce their risk of developing a number of chronic diseases, including diabetes, obesity, and heart disease. It is crucial to bear in mind that different kinds of physical exercise each bring their own own collection of benefits, and it is essential to remember this fact. Strength training, for instance, may contribute to an increase in muscle mass and bone density, whilst aerobic exercise may contribute to an improvement in cardiovascular health and endurance. Exercising regularly is a great way to attain both of these advantages.

When it comes to reducing inflammation, in addition to the strategies that were covered before, there are a number of other ways that have the potential to be beneficial. These strategies include: Consuming foods that are high in omega-3 fatty acids, such nuts and fish, may be one way to help reduce inflammation throughout the body. [More citation is required] It has been shown that omega-3 fatty acids have anti-inflammatory qualities, and it is probable that they also assist in the process of lowering the chance of acquiring chronic diseases such as cardiovascular disease and arthritis.

One further way for decreasing inflammatory reactions in the body is to avoid or minimize exposure to environmental toxins such as air pollution, pesticides, and chemicals. This may help reduce the severity of the inflammatory responses. The exposure to these chemicals also carries with it the possibility of causing inflammation, in addition to elevating the chance of acquiring chronic diseases. In addition, it is of the utmost importance to address any underlying health conditions, such as diabetes, obesity, or autoimmune disorders, which may be contributing factors in the development of inflammation if they are not already being done so.

Lastly, but certainly not least, maintaining a positive outlook on life and a sound frame of mind may also help to contribute to a decrease in inflammation. According to the results of a number of studies, inflammation may be brought on by both chronic stress and negative emotions, but it is something that can be alleviated by both positive emotions and a sense that one's life has some kind of purpose. Finding ways to produce positive sentiments and a sense of purpose may be beneficial for one's physical as well as mental health, and one way to do so is through learning new skills. Volunteering, spending time with loved ones, and indulging in hobbies are some examples of the kinds of activities that might accomplish this goal.

Reducing levels of inflammation is one of the most significant components of leading a healthy lifestyle, which is one of the most important aspects of leading a healthy lifestyle generally. If we make it a regular part of our routine to participate in healthy activities like physical exercise, strategies for stress management, and nutritional eating, we may be able to reduce inflammation and produce a healthier body. In conclusion, keep in mind that in order to live a happy and healthy life, you need to take care of both your physical body and your mental state.

COOKBOOK

Z

BREAKFAST

1. Omelette with spinach and feta cheese

2. Scrambled eggs with tomatoes and avocado

3. Greek yogurt with low FODMAP fruits and gluten-free granola

4. Gluten-free toast with peanut butter and banana

5. Breakfast smoothie with low FODMAP fruits, spinach, and almond milk

6. Gluten-free oatmeal with strawberries and almond butter

7. Rice cake with tuna and cucumber

8. Gluten-free toast with smoked salmon and cream cheese

9. Egg muffins with spinach and cheese

10. Breakfast burrito with scrambled eggs, peppers, and bacon

11. Rice cakes with almond butter and blueberries

12. Gluten-free granola with yogurt and low FODMAP fruits

13. Breakfast hash with sweet potatoes, peppers, and sausage

14. Gluten-free pancakes with blueberries and maple syrup

15. Shakshuka with tomato, bell pepper, and eggs

16. Chia seed pudding with low FODMAP fruits and coconut milk

17. Gluten-free waffles with strawberries and whipped cream

18. Breakfast bowl with quinoa, scrambled eggs, and avocado

19. Rice cake with turkey, lettuce, and tomato

20. Gluten-free toast with scrambled eggs and bacon

21. Breakfast sandwich with gluten-free bread, egg, and ham

22. Frittata with spinach, tomatoes, and goat cheese

23. Greek yogurt with low FODMAP fruits and walnuts

24. Gluten-free oatmeal with raspberries and almonds

25. Breakfast burrito with black beans, scrambled eggs, and cheese

OMELETTE WITH SPINACH AND FETA CHEESE

SERVINGS: 1

PREPARATION TIME: 10 minutes

INGREDIENTS:

- 2 large eggs

- 1 tablespoon lactose-free milk

- Salt and pepper to taste

- 1 teaspoon garlic-infused oil

- 1/2 cup fresh spinach leaves

- 1/4 cup crumbled feta cheese

INSTRUCTIONS:

In a small bowl, whisk together the eggs, lactose-free milk, salt, and pepper.

Heat the garlic-infused oil in a small non-stick skillet over medium heat.

Add the spinach leaves to the skillet and cook for 1-2 minutes or until wilted.

Pour the egg mixture into the skillet and let it cook for 2-3 minutes or until the edges start to set.

Using a spatula, gently lift the edges of the omelette and let the uncooked egg flow underneath.

When the omelette is almost set, sprinkle the crumbled feta cheese over one side.

Use the spatula to fold the other side of the omelette over the cheese-filled side.

Cook for an additional minute or until the cheese is melted and the eggs are fully cooked.

Serve hot.

Calorie and Macro (Carbs, Prot, Fat):

This recipe contains approximately 265 calories, 20g protein, 18g fat,

SCRAMBLED EGGS WITH TOMATOES AND AVOCADO

SERVINGS: 2

PREPARATION TIME: 10 minutes

INGREDIENTS:

- 4 eggs

- 1 medium tomato, diced

- 1/2 avocado, diced

- 1 tablespoon garlic-infused oil

- Salt and pepper to taste

INSTRUCTIONS:

Crack the eggs into a bowl and whisk until well combined.

Heat the garlic-infused oil in a nonstick skillet over medium heat.

Add the diced tomato to the skillet and sauté for 2-3 minutes or until the tomato is slightly softened.

Pour the eggs into the skillet with the tomato and stir gently.

Cook the eggs, stirring occasionally, until they are scrambled and cooked through, about 3-5 minutes.

Remove the skillet from the heat and stir in the diced avocado.

Season with salt and pepper to taste.

Serve the scrambled eggs hot.

CALORIES AND MACROS (CARBS, PROT, FAT)

Calories: 274 per serving

Carbs: 6g

Protein: 16g

Fat: 21g

GLUTEN-FREE YOGURT PARFAIT WITH LOW FODMAP FRUITS AND GRANOLA

SERVINGS: 1

PREPARATION TIME: 5 minutes

INGREDIENTS:

1/2 cup gluten-free granola

1/2 cup lactose-free Greek yogurt

1/2 cup low FODMAP fruits (such as blueberries, raspberries, or strawberries)

1 tablespoon chia seeds (optional)

INSTRUCTIONS:

In a small bowl or glass, layer the gluten-free granola, lactose-free Greek yogurt, and low FODMAP fruits.

Repeat the layering until you reach the top of the bowl or glass.

Top with chia seeds, if desired.

Serve immediately.

CALORIES AND MACROS:

This recipe provides approximately 340 calories, 47 grams of carbohydrates, 19 grams of protein, and 8 grams of fat. The exact nutritional information may vary depending on the specific INGREDIENTS and brands used.

GLUTEN-FREE TOAST WITH PEANUT BUTTER AND BANANA

SERVINGS: 1

PREPARATION TIME: 5 minutes

INGREDIENTS:

2 slices gluten-free bread

1 tablespoon peanut butter (check for no added FODMAP INGREDIENTS)

1 small ripe banana, sliced

Optional: a drizzle of honey (for sweetness)

INSTRUCTIONS:

Toast the gluten-free bread slices until golden brown.

Spread the peanut butter evenly over each slice of toasted bread.

Place the sliced banana on top of the peanut butter on one slice of bread.

Drizzle a small amount of honey over the banana if desired.

Place the other slice of bread on top to make a sandwich.

Serve and enjoy!

CALORIE AND MACRO (CARBS, PROT, FAT):

Calories: 360

Carbohydrates: 59g

Protein: 11g

Fat: 12g

Note: The nutritional information may vary depending on the brand of bread and peanut butter used.

BREAKFAST SMOOTHIE WITH LOW FODMAP FRUITS, SPINACH, AND ALMOND MILK

SERVINGS: 1

PREPARATION TIME: 5 minutes

INGREDIENTS:

1/2 cup low FODMAP fruits (such as strawberries, blueberries, or raspberries)

1 handful baby spinach leaves

1/2 banana

1 cup unsweetened almond milk

1 tablespoon chia seeds

1/4 teaspoon vanilla extract

Ice (optional)

INSTRUCTIONS:

Add the low FODMAP fruits, baby spinach leaves, and banana to a blender.

Pour in the almond milk, chia seeds, and vanilla extract.

If desired, add a few ice cubes to the blender for a chilled smoothie.

Blend all the INGREDIENTS until smooth and well combined.

Pour the smoothie into a glass and serve immediately.

CALORIE AND MACRO (CARBS, PROT, FAT)

Calories: 187

Carbohydrates: 27g

Protein: 6g

Fat: 7g

GLUTEN-FREE OATMEAL WITH STRAWBERRIES AND ALMOND BUTTER

SERVINGS: 1

PREPARATION TIME: 10 minutes

INGREDIENTS:

1/2 cup gluten-free rolled oats

1 cup water

1/2 cup sliced strawberries

1 tablespoon almond butter

1 teaspoon honey

1/2 teaspoon cinnamon

INSTRUCTIONS:

In a small pot, bring 1 cup of water to a boil.

Add the gluten-free rolled oats to the boiling water and reduce the heat to low.

Cook the oats for 5-7 minutes, stirring occasionally, until they are thick and creamy.

Remove the pot from the heat and stir in the sliced strawberries, almond butter, honey, and cinnamon.

Serve the oatmeal in a bowl and top with additional sliced strawberries and a drizzle of almond butter, if desired.

Calories and Macro-nutrients (per serving):

Calories: 335

Carbohydrates: 45g

Protein: 9g

Fat: 14g

RICE CAKE WITH TUNA AND CUCUMBER

SERVINGS: 1

PREPARATION TIME: 5 minutes

INGREDIENTS:

1 rice cake

1 can of tuna (in water), drained

2 tablespoons of mayonnaise

1/4 cup of chopped cucumber

Salt and pepper to taste

INSTRUCTIONS:

In a small bowl, mix the drained tuna with the mayonnaise until well combined.

Add the chopped cucumber to the tuna mixture and mix well.

Season with salt and pepper to taste.

Spread the tuna mixture over the rice cake.

Serve immediately.

Calorie and Macro (Carbs, Prot, Fat):

Calories: 290

Carbs: 11g

Protein: 25g

Fat: 15g

GLUTEN-FREE TOAST WITH SMOKED SALMON AND CREAM CHEESE

SERVINGS: 1

PREPARATION TIME: 5 minutes

INGREDIENTS:

2 slices of gluten-free bread

2 tablespoons of cream cheese

2 oz of smoked salmon

1 tablespoon of chopped chives

Salt and pepper to taste

INSTRUCTIONS:

Toast the gluten-free bread slices to your desired level of crispiness.

Spread 1 tablespoon of cream cheese on each slice of toast.

Top each slice with 1 oz of smoked salmon.

Sprinkle chopped chives on top of the smoked salmon.

Season with salt and pepper to taste.

Serve immediately and enjoy!

CALORIES AND MACROS (CARBS, PROTEIN, FAT):

Calories: 380

Carbohydrates: 38g

Protein: 24g

Fat: 14g

Note: Nutritional values may vary depending on the brand of INGREDIENTS used.

EGG MUFFINS WITH SPINACH AND CHEESE

SERVINGS: 6 muffins

PREPARATION TIME: 10 minutes

INGREDIENTS:

6 large eggs

1/4 cup unsweetened almond milk

1/2 teaspoon garlic powder

1/2 teaspoon onion powder

1/2 teaspoon dried basil

Salt and pepper, to taste

2 cups fresh spinach, chopped

1/2 cup shredded cheddar cheese

INSTRUCTIONS:

Preheat the oven to 350°F (175°C).

In a large mixing bowl, whisk together the eggs, almond milk, garlic powder, onion powder, dried basil, salt, and pepper.

Add the chopped spinach and shredded cheddar cheese to the bowl and mix well.

Grease a muffin tin with non-stick cooking spray.

Pour the egg mixture evenly into the muffin cups.

Bake the egg muffins for 20-25 minutes, or until the tops are golden brown and a toothpick inserted into the center of a muffin comes out clean.

Let the muffins cool for a few minutes before removing them from the muffin tin and serving.

CALORIES AND MACROS PER SERVING:

Each egg muffin contains approximately 119 calories, 8g protein, 2g carbohydrates, and 9g fat.

BREAKFAST BURRITO WITH SCRAMBLED EGGS, PEPPERS, AND BACON

SERVINGS: 2

PREPARATION TIME: 20 minutes

INGREDIENTS:

4 gluten-free tortillas

4 large eggs

2 strips of bacon, diced

1/2 red bell pepper, sliced

1/2 green bell pepper, sliced

2 tablespoons garlic-infused oil

Salt and pepper to taste

INSTRUCTIONS:

In a large skillet, cook the diced bacon over medium-high heat until crispy. Remove from the skillet and set aside on a paper towel to drain excess grease.

In the same skillet, add the sliced bell peppers and cook over medium-high heat until tender-crisp. Remove from the skillet and set aside.

Crack the eggs into a bowl and whisk until well beaten.

Heat the garlic-infused oil in the skillet over medium heat. Add the eggs to the skillet and cook, stirring occasionally, until scrambled and cooked through.

Warm the gluten-free tortillas in the microwave or on a skillet until soft and pliable.

To assemble the burritos, divide the scrambled eggs, bacon, and bell peppers among the tortillas. Roll up the tortillas tightly and serve immediately.

NUTRITION INFORMATION (per serving):

Calories: 462

Carbohydrates: 41g

Protein: 16g

Fat: 27g

CHIA SEED PUDDING WITH LOW FODMAP FRUITS AND COCONUT MILK

SERVINGS: 2

PREPARATION TIME: 10 minutes + overnight chilling

INGREDIENTS:

1/4 cup chia seeds

1 cup low FODMAP coconut milk

1 tablespoon maple syrup

1/2 teaspoon vanilla extract

1/2 cup low FODMAP fruits (such as strawberries, blueberries, or raspberries)

INSTRUCTIONS:

In a medium bowl, whisk together the chia seeds, coconut milk, maple syrup, and vanilla extract until well combined.

Stir in the low FODMAP fruits.

Cover the bowl with plastic wrap and refrigerate overnight or for at least 4 hours to allow the chia seeds to thicken and absorb the liquid.

Once the chia seed pudding has chilled and thickened, stir it well to break up any clumps and distribute the fruit evenly.

Divide the pudding between two serving dishes and top with additional low FODMAP fruits, if desired.

CALORIES AND MACROS:

One serving of this chia seed pudding with low FODMAP fruits and coconut milk contains approximately:

250 calories

19 grams of carbohydrates

5 grams of protein

18 grams of fat

GLUTEN-FREE GRANOLA WITH YOGURT AND LOW FODMAP FRUITS

SERVINGS: 2

PREPARATION TIME: 15 minutes

INGREDIENTS:

1/2 cup gluten-free rolled oats

1/4 cup unsweetened shredded coconut

2 tablespoons chopped pecans

1 tablespoon maple syrup

1 tablespoon coconut oil

1/4 teaspoon ground cinnamon

Pinch of salt

1 cup lactose-free yogurt

1/2 cup low FODMAP fruits (e.g., strawberries, blueberries, raspberries)

INSTRUCTIONS:

Preheat the oven to 325°F (160°C).

In a mixing bowl, combine the gluten-free rolled oats, unsweetened shredded coconut, chopped pecans, maple syrup, coconut oil, ground cinnamon, and a pinch of salt.

Mix everything together until the oats are coated with the maple syrup and coconut oil.

Spread the mixture onto a baking sheet lined with parchment paper.

Bake for 10-12 minutes or until the granola is golden brown, stirring occasionally to prevent burning.

Remove the baking sheet from the oven and let the granola cool completely.

To assemble the breakfast bowls, divide the lactose-free yogurt between two bowls.

Top each bowl with the low FODMAP fruits and the cooled granola.

Serve and enjoy!

CALORIE AND MACRO (CARBS, PROT, FAT):

Calories: 350

Carbohydrates: 32g

Protein: 15g

Fat: 20g

BREAKFAST HASH WITH SWEET POTATOES, PEPPERS, AND SAUSAGE

SERVINGS: 4

PREPARATION TIME: 30 minutes

INGREDIENTS:

2 large sweet potatoes, peeled and diced into 1/2 inch cubes

2 tablespoons olive oil

1/2 teaspoon paprika

1/2 teaspoon garlic powder

Salt and pepper to taste

1 red bell pepper, diced

1 green bell pepper, diced

1 yellow onion, diced

4 gluten-free sausages, sliced into rounds

4 eggs

INSTRUCTIONS:

Preheat the oven to 425°F.

Toss the sweet potato cubes with the olive oil, paprika, garlic powder, salt, and pepper in a large bowl until evenly coated.

Spread the seasoned sweet potatoes out in a single layer on a baking sheet.

Roast the sweet potatoes in the preheated oven for 20-25 minutes or until tender and lightly browned.

While the sweet potatoes are roasting, heat a large skillet over medium-high heat.

Add the diced bell peppers and onion to the skillet and sauté for 5-7 minutes or until softened.

Add the sliced sausage to the skillet and sauté for an additional 3-4 minutes or until lightly browned.

Divide the roasted sweet potatoes among four plates.

Top each plate with the sausage and pepper mixture.

Fry the eggs to your liking and place one egg on top of each plate.

Serve immediately.

CALORIES AND MACROS PER SERVING:

Calories: 440

Carbs: 33g

Protein: 19g

Fat: 27g

GLUTEN-FREE PANCAKES WITH BLUEBERRIES AND MAPLE SYRUP

SERVINGS: 4

PREPARATION TIME: 20 minutes

INGREDIENTS:

1 cup gluten-free all-purpose flour

2 tablespoons sugar

2 teaspoons baking powder

1/4 teaspoon salt

1 cup almond milk

2 tablespoons vegetable oil

1 large egg

1/2 cup fresh blueberries

Maple syrup for serving

INSTRUCTIONS:

In a large bowl, whisk together the gluten-free flour, sugar, baking powder, and salt.

In a separate bowl, whisk together the almond milk, vegetable oil, and egg.

Pour the wet INGREDIENTS into the dry INGREDIENTS and stir until just combined.

Fold in the blueberries.

Heat a non-stick skillet or griddle over medium-high heat.

Scoop 1/4 cup of the pancake batter onto the skillet for each pancake.

Cook for 2-3 minutes on each side or until golden brown.

Repeat with the remaining batter, adding more oil to the skillet as needed.

Serve the pancakes with maple syrup.

CALORIE AND MACRO (CARBS, PROT, FAT):

Calories: 267

Carbohydrates: 38g

Protein: 4g

Fat: 11g

SHAKSHUKA WITH TOMATO, BELL PEPPER, AND EGGS

SERVINGS: 4

PREPARATION TIME: 10 minutes

COOKING TIME: 25 minutes

INGREDIENTS:

2 tablespoons olive oil

1 red bell pepper, diced

1 yellow onion, diced

3 garlic cloves, minced

1 teaspoon smoked paprika

1/2 teaspoon ground cumin

1/4 teaspoon red pepper flakes

1 (28-ounce) can whole peeled tomatoes, crushed by hand

Salt and freshly ground black pepper

4-8 eggs

Chopped fresh parsley or cilantro, for garnish

INSTRUCTIONS:

Heat the olive oil in a large skillet over medium-high heat.

Add the diced bell pepper and onion and cook until softened, about 5-7 minutes.

Add the minced garlic, smoked paprika, ground cumin, and red pepper flakes, and cook for another 1-2 minutes until fragrant.

Add the crushed tomatoes and season with salt and black pepper to taste.

Simmer the tomato sauce over medium-low heat for 10-15 minutes, until it has thickened slightly.

Using a spoon, create small wells in the tomato sauce and crack an egg into each well.

Cover the skillet and let the eggs cook for 8-10 minutes, until the whites are set and the yolks are still runny.

Garnish with chopped fresh parsley or cilantro and serve hot.

CALORIE AND MACRO (CARBS, PROT, FAT):

Calories: 183

Carbohydrates: 12g

Protein: 9g

Fat: 12g

CHIA SEED PUDDING WITH LOW FODMAP FRUITS AND COCONUT MILK

SERVINGS: 2

PREPARATION TIME: 10 minutes

INGREDIENTS:

1/4 cup chia seeds

1 cup unsweetened coconut milk

1 tablespoon maple syrup

1/4 teaspoon vanilla extract

1/2 cup low FODMAP fruits (e.g. strawberries, blueberries, kiwi, banana)

2 tablespoons unsweetened shredded coconut

INSTRUCTIONS:

In a small bowl, whisk together the chia seeds, coconut milk, maple syrup, and vanilla extract.

Let the mixture sit for at least 5 minutes to thicken up, stirring occasionally.

In the meantime, slice the low FODMAP fruits.

Once the chia seed mixture has thickened to a pudding-like consistency, divide it between two small bowls.

Top each bowl with sliced low FODMAP fruits and unsweetened shredded coconut.

Serve immediately or chill in the refrigerator for later.

Calories and Macro (Carbs, Prot, Fat):

Per serving:

Calories: 212

Carbs: 20g

Protein: 4g

Fat: 14g

GLUTEN-FREE WAFFLES WITH STRAWBERRIES AND WHIPPED CREAM

SERVINGS: 4

PREPARATION TIME: 20 minutes

INGREDIENTS:

1 1/2 cups gluten-free all-purpose flour

1 tablespoon baking powder

1/4 teaspoon salt

1 tablespoon sugar

2 eggs, separated

1 1/2 cups almond milk

1/4 cup vegetable oil

1 teaspoon vanilla extract

1 cup fresh strawberries, sliced

1/2 cup whipped cream

INSTRUCTIONS:

In a large bowl, whisk together the gluten-free flour, baking powder, salt, and sugar.

In a separate bowl, beat the egg whites until stiff peaks form.

In a small bowl, whisk together the egg yolks, almond milk, vegetable oil, and vanilla extract.

Add the wet INGREDIENTS to the dry INGREDIENTS and stir until well combined.

Gently fold in the beaten egg whites until just incorporated.

Preheat a waffle iron and spray with cooking spray.

Pour the batter into the waffle iron and cook according to the manufacturer's INSTRUCTIONS.

Serve the waffles topped with sliced strawberries and whipped cream.

NUTRITION INFORMATION PER SERVING:

Calories: 370

Carbohydrates: 36g, Protein: 8g, Fat: 23g

QUINOA BREAKFAST BOWL WITH SCRAMBLED EGGS AND AVOCADO

SERVINGS: 1

PREPARATION TIME: 15 minutes

INGREDIENTS:

1/2 cup cooked quinoa

2 large eggs

1/4 avocado, sliced

1/4 cup diced red bell pepper

1/4 cup diced zucchini

1/4 cup chopped spinach

1/4 tsp. salt

1/4 tsp. black pepper

1 tbsp. olive oil

INSTRUCTIONS:

In a medium skillet, heat olive oil over medium heat.

Add the red bell pepper, zucchini, and spinach to the skillet and sauté for 2-3 minutes, until the vegetables are tender.

Add the cooked quinoa to the skillet and stir well to combine with the vegetables. Season with salt and black pepper.

In a separate bowl, beat the eggs with a fork.

Pour the eggs into the skillet with the quinoa and vegetables, stirring constantly until the eggs are cooked through.

Transfer the quinoa and egg mixture to a bowl and top with sliced avocado.

Serve hot and enjoy!

Calories and Macro:

Calories: 442

Carbs: 34g

Protein: 20g

Fat: 25g

AVOCADO AND QUINOA BREAKFAST BOWL

SERVINGS: 1

PREPARATION TIME: 20 minutes

INGREDIENTS:

1/2 cup quinoa, rinsed

1 cup water

1/2 avocado, sliced

1 small tomato, chopped

1 scallion, sliced

1/4 cup canned black beans, drained and rinsed

1/4 teaspoon ground cumin

1/4 teaspoon smoked paprika

Salt and pepper to taste

1 tablespoon olive oil

1 egg

1 teaspoon white vinegar

1/4 cup fresh spinach leaves

INSTRUCTIONS:

In a medium saucepan, combine the quinoa and water. Bring to a boil, then reduce heat to low and cover. Cook for 15 minutes or until the water is absorbed and the quinoa is tender.

In a small bowl, combine the avocado, tomato, and scallion. Set aside.

In a small skillet, heat the black beans with the cumin, smoked paprika, and a pinch of salt and pepper. Cook for 2-3 minutes, stirring occasionally.

In another small skillet, heat the olive oil over medium heat. Crack the egg into the skillet and fry until the white is set but the yolk is still runny.

While the egg is cooking, bring a small pot of water to a boil. Add the white vinegar and stir. Reduce the heat to low and gently crack the egg into the water. Cook for 2-3 minutes or until the white is set but the yolk is still runny.

To assemble the breakfast bowl, start with a bed of fresh spinach leaves. Top with the cooked quinoa, black beans, and avocado mixture. Place the fried egg on top of the avocado mixture, and then add the poached egg on top of the fried egg.

Season with salt and pepper to taste.

CALORIES AND MACROS (CARBS, PROT, FAT):

Calories: 476

Carbs: 43g

Protein: 16g

Fat: 29g

BREAKFAST SANDWICH WITH GLUTEN-FREE BREAD, EGG, AND BACON

SERVINGS: 1

PREPARATION TIME: 10 minutes

INGREDIENTS:

2 slices gluten-free bread

2 slices of bacon

1 egg

Salt and pepper to taste

1 tablespoon of butter

Optional: lettuce, tomato, avocado

INSTRUCTIONS:

Cook the bacon in a non-stick pan until crispy. Remove from pan and set aside.

In the same pan, melt the butter over medium heat.

Crack the egg into the pan and cook until the whites are set but the yolk is still runny, about 2-3 minutes. Sprinkle with salt and pepper.

Toast the gluten-free bread.

Assemble the sandwich by placing the cooked egg and bacon between the slices of toast. Add lettuce, tomato, and avocado if desired.

Serve immediately.

CALORIE AND MACRO (CARBS, PROT, FAT):

Calories: 435

Carbs: 36g

Protein: 22g

Fat: 23g

Note: Nutritional values may vary depending on the specific INGREDIENTS used.

HAM, EGG, AND CHEESE BREAKFAST SANDWICH

SERVINGS: 1

PREPARATION TIME: 10 minutes

INGREDIENTS:

1 gluten-free English muffin

1 slice of ham

1 large egg

1 slice of cheddar cheese

1 tablespoon of unsalted butter

Salt and pepper, to taste

INSTRUCTIONS:

Preheat a nonstick skillet over medium heat.

Slice the English muffin in half and toast it.

While the muffin is toasting, add the butter to the skillet and let it melt.

Crack the egg into the skillet and cook to your desired doneness.

Season the egg with salt and pepper.

Place the ham on one half of the toasted muffin and top with the cooked egg.

Add the cheddar cheese slice on top of the egg.

Cover the sandwich with the other half of the toasted muffin.

Serve immediately and enjoy!

CALORIE AND MACRO (CARBS, PROT, FAT):

Calories: 410

Carbs: 29g

Protein: 23g

Fat: 22g

SPINACH, TOMATO, AND GOAT CHEESE FRITTATA

SERVINGS: 4

PREPARATION TIME: 10 minutes

COOK TIME: 20 minutes

INGREDIENTS:

8 large eggs

1/2 cup lactose-free milk

1 tablespoon garlic-infused oil

2 cups fresh baby spinach

1 cup chopped cherry tomatoes

2 ounces crumbled goat cheese

Salt and pepper, to taste

INSTRUCTIONS:

Preheat the oven to 375°F (190°C).

In a large bowl, whisk together the eggs and lactose-free milk. Set aside.

Heat the garlic-infused oil in a 10-inch oven-safe skillet over medium heat.

Add the spinach and cook until wilted, stirring occasionally.

Add the chopped cherry tomatoes to the skillet and cook for 1-2 minutes.

Pour the egg mixture over the spinach and tomatoes in the skillet.

Sprinkle crumbled goat cheese over the top.

Cook the frittata over medium heat for 5-6 minutes or until the edges start to set.

Transfer the skillet to the preheated oven and bake for 10-12 minutes or until the frittata is set and the top is golden.

Remove from the oven and let it cool for a few minutes before slicing and serving.

Season with salt and pepper, to taste.

CALORIE AND MACRO (CARBS, PROT, FAT):

Calories: 214

Carbohydrates: 3g

Protein: 18g

Fat: 15g

GREEK YOGURT WITH LOW FODMAP FRUITS AND WALNUTS

2 SERVINGS

PREPARATION TIME: 5 minutes

INGREDIENTS:

2 cups of lactose-free Greek yogurt

1 cup of low FODMAP fruits (e.g. strawberries, blueberries, kiwi, oranges)

1/4 cup of chopped walnuts

1 tablespoon of maple syrup (optional)

INSTRUCTIONS:

Divide the Greek yogurt evenly between two bowls.

Wash and chop the low FODMAP fruits of your choice and place them on top of the yogurt.

Sprinkle the chopped walnuts over the fruit.

Drizzle with maple syrup if desired.

Serve and enjoy!

Calories and Macro (carbs, prot, fat) per serving:

Calories: 297

Carbohydrates: 23g

Protein: 19g

Fat: 14g

GLUTEN-FREE OATMEAL WITH RASPBERRIES AND ALMONDS

SERVINGS: 1

PREPARATION TIME: 10 minutes

INGREDIENTS:

1/2 cup gluten-free oats

1 cup almond milk

1/4 cup fresh raspberries

1 tbsp sliced almonds

1 tbsp maple syrup

INSTRUCTIONS:

In a small saucepan, bring almond milk to a simmer over medium heat.

Add gluten-free oats and stir to combine.

Cook for 5-7 minutes or until the oatmeal has thickened, stirring occasionally.

Remove from heat and let cool for a minute.

Top with fresh raspberries, sliced almonds, and a drizzle of maple syrup.

Enjoy!

Calories and Macro (Carbs, Prot, Fat):

Calories: 305

Carbs: 49g

Protein: 9g

Fat: 8g

LUNCH

1. Grilled chicken with roasted vegetables

2. Tuna salad lettuce wraps

3. Low FODMAP vegetable stir-fry with rice

4. Turkey and lettuce wrap

5. Low FODMAP chicken and vegetable skewers

6. Grilled salmon with roasted sweet potato

7. Low FODMAP sushi rolls with crab and cucumber

8. Steak salad with low FODMAP veggies

9. Baked sweet potato with low FODMAP toppings

10. Low FODMAP Greek salad with feta cheese

11. Chicken and vegetable kebabs with quinoa

12. Low FODMAP chicken and vegetable stir-fry with rice noodles

13. Turkey burger with low FODMAP toppings

14. Grilled shrimp with quinoa salad

15. Low FODMAP chicken Caesar salad

16. Baked salmon with roasted vegetables

17. Low FODMAP chicken and vegetable skewers with quinoa

18. Turkey lettuce wraps with low FODMAP dipping sauce

19. Grilled chicken with low FODMAP vegetables and brown rice

20. Low FODMAP tuna and avocado salad

21. Chicken and vegetable kabobs with brown rice

22. Baked sweet potato with low FODMAP tuna salad

23. Grilled shrimp and vegetable skewers with quinoa salad

24. Low FODMAP chicken and vegetable stir-fry with quinoa

25. Turkey and cheese lettuce wraps with low FODMAP toppings

GRILLED CHICKEN WITH ROASTED VEGETABLES

4 SERVINGS

PREPARATION TIME: 30 minutes

INGREDIENTS:

4 boneless, skinless chicken breasts

2 bell peppers, sliced

1 zucchini, sliced

1 eggplant, sliced

2 tbsp olive oil

Salt and pepper to taste

INSTRUCTIONS:

Prepare a grill with medium-high heat.

Rub salt and pepper onto both sides of the chicken breasts.

Season veggies with salt and pepper and brush with olive oil.

Fire up the grill, and cook the chicken for 6 to 8 minutes each side, or until it reaches an internal temperature of 165 degrees.

Roast the veggies at 400 degrees Fahrenheit for 15 to 20 minutes, or until soft, while the chicken is in the oven.

Prepare the roasted veggies and serve them beside the chicken.

CALORIE AND MACRO (CARBS, PROT, FAT):

Calories: 290

Carbs: 9g

Protein: 38g

Fat: 11g

TUNA SALAD LETTUCE WRAPS

SERVINGS: 2

PREPARATION TIME: 15 minutes

INGREDIENTS:

1 can of low FODMAP tuna, drained

1/4 cup of mayonnaise

1 tablespoon of Dijon mustard

2 tablespoons of chopped scallions (green part only)

Salt and pepper to taste

4 large lettuce leaves

1/2 cup of sliced cucumber

1/2 cup of shredded carrots

INSTRUCTIONS:

Combine the tuna that has been drained, the mayonnaise, the Dijon mustard, and the chopped scallions in a small mixing dish. Combine thoroughly.

Salt and pepper may be added to taste as a seasoning.

Arrange the lettuce leaves on a dish, and then dollop the tuna salad on top of each individual leaf.

Sliced cucumber and shredded carrots should be placed on top of each lettuce wrap.

Wrap the ingredients in the lettuce leaves, and serve them up right away.

CALORIE AND MACRO (CARBS, PROT, FAT):

Calories: 219 per serving

Carbohydrates: 5g

Protein: 18g

81

Fat: 14g

BLACK BEAN, SCRAMBLED EGG, AND CHEESE BREAKFAST BURRITO

SERVINGS: 1

PREPARATION TIME: 15 minutes

INGREDIENTS:

1 gluten-free tortilla

1/2 cup canned black beans, rinsed and drained

2 eggs, scrambled

1/4 cup shredded cheddar cheese

1/4 cup salsa

1 tablespoon chopped fresh cilantro (optional)

INSTRUCTIONS:

In the microwave, heat the tortilla for about ten to fifteen seconds, or until it is malleable.

The black beans should be positioned in the middle of the tortilla.

On top of the black beans, add the eggs that have been scrambled.

The eggs would benefit with a topping of shredded cheddar cheese.

Place a dollop of salsa on top of the cheese.

If you want, you may sprinkle some chopped cilantro on top.

To make a burrito shape, roll up the tortilla and tuck in the edges to produce the shape of a burrito.

Immediately serve after cooking.

CALORIE AND MACRO (CARBS, PROT, FAT):

Calories: 422

Carbohydrates: 36g

Protein: 27g

Fat: 19g

LOW FODMAP VEGETABLE STIR-FRY WITH RICE

SERVINGS: 4

PREPARATION TIME: 25 minutes

INGREDIENTS:

2 cups cooked brown rice

1 tablespoon garlic-infused oil

2 small zucchinis, sliced

2 small carrots, sliced

1/2 red bell pepper, sliced

1/2 cup green beans, trimmed and halved

1 tablespoon grated fresh ginger

2 tablespoons low-sodium soy sauce

1 tablespoon rice vinegar

Salt and pepper, to taste

INSTRUCTIONS:

Warm the oil that has been flavored with garlic in a wok or a big frying pan over medium-high heat.

After adding the zucchini, carrots, red bell pepper, and green beans to the pan, stir-fry them for three to five minutes, or until the veggies have reached the desired texture.

Stir-frying will continue for one more minute once grated ginger is added to the pan.

Combine the low-sodium soy sauce and rice vinegar in a small bowl and mix together until smooth.

Once the rice is finished cooking, add it to the pan with the veggies and toss to mix everything.

After pouring the soy sauce mixture over the rice and veggies, toss everything together to ensure that it is distributed evenly.

Salt and pepper may be added to taste as a seasoning.

To be served hot.

CALORIE AND MACRO (CARBS, PROT, FAT):

Calories: 215

Carbohydrates: 41g

Protein: 6g, Fat: 3g

TURKEY AND LETTUCE WRAP

SERVINGS: 2

PREPARATION TIME: 15 minutes

INGREDIENTS:

4 large lettuce leaves

8 oz cooked turkey breast, sliced

1/2 red bell pepper, sliced

1/2 cucumber, sliced

1/2 avocado, sliced

2 tbsp low FODMAP mayonnaise

1 tbsp Dijon mustard

Salt and pepper, to taste

INSTRUCTIONS:

Spread the lettuce leaves out on a surface that has been well cleaned.

Mayonnaise and Dijon mustard should be combined in a low-volume container first.

On the lettuce leaves, spread the mayonnaise and mustard mixture that has been combined.

Sliced turkey, red bell pepper, cucumber, and avocado should be placed on top of each leaf of lettuce.

The desired amount of salt and pepper should be sprinkled on top.

Wrap each individual lettuce leaf like a wrap and then serve.

CALORIE AND MACRO (CARBS, PROT, FAT):

Calories per serving: 266

Carbohydrates: 7g

Protein: 33g

Fat: 12g

LOW FODMAP CHICKEN AND VEGETABLE SKEWERS

SERVINGS: 4

PREPARATION TIME: 30 minutes

INGREDIENTS:

2 boneless, skinless chicken breasts, cut into 1-inch cubes

1 red bell pepper, seeded and cut into 1-inch pieces

1 zucchini, sliced into 1-inch rounds

1 tablespoon garlic-infused olive oil

1 tablespoon lemon juice

1 teaspoon dried oregano

Salt and black pepper, to taste

Wooden skewers

INSTRUCTIONS:

Prepare the grill or grill pan by heating it to a medium-high temperature.

Olive oil that has been infused with garlic is combined with lemon juice, dried oregano, salt, and black pepper in a large bowl with a whisk.

After adding the chicken, bell pepper, and zucchini to the bowl, mix everything together so that the marinade evenly coats the veggies as well as the chicken.

Skewer the chicken and veggies on the wooden skewers in a manner that alternates between the two ingredients.

Cook the skewers over a grill for ten to twelve minutes, turning them every so often, until the chicken is completely cooked through and the veggies are soft but still have a charred flavor.

Warm the skewers and accompany them with a salad or rice on the side.

CALORIE AND MACRO (CARBS, PROT, FAT):

Per serving - Calories: 170

Carbohydrates: 5g

Protein: 26g, Fat: 5g

GRILLED SALMON WITH ROASTED SWEET POTATO

SERVINGS: 2

PREPARATION TIME: 40 minutes

INGREDIENTS:

2 salmon fillets

2 medium sweet potatoes, peeled and cubed

2 tbsp olive oil

1 tbsp maple syrup

1 tbsp low FODMAP soy sauce

1 tsp grated ginger

1 tsp minced garlic

Salt and pepper to taste

Fresh parsley for garnish

INSTRUCTIONS:

Turn the temperature on the oven to 400 degrees Fahrenheit (200 degrees Celsius).

Mix the sweet potatoes with a dash of salt and pepper, along with a tablespoon of olive oil. Roast them in the oven for 25 to 30 minutes, or until they are soft and have a little browning on them. Spread them out in a single layer on a baking sheet.

In the meanwhile, combine the remaining tablespoon of olive oil, the remaining tablespoon of maple syrup, the remaining tablespoon of soy sauce, ginger, and garlic. The salmon fillets should be seasoned with salt and pepper, and then the seasoning combination should be brushed over both sides of the fillets.

Prepare a grill pan by heating it over a medium-high flame. Add the salmon fillets and cook for three to four minutes on each side, or until they have reached the amount of doneness that you choose.

Salmon that has been grilled should be served with sweet potatoes that have been baked and topped with fresh parsley.

CALORIE AND MACRO (CARBS, PROT, FAT):

Calories: 375

Carbs: 25g

Protein: 28g, Fat: 18g

LOW FODMAP SUSHI ROLLS WITH CRAB AND CUCUMBER

SERVINGS: 4

PREPARATION TIME: 30 minutes

INGREDIENTS:

4 sheets of nori seaweed

2 cups of sushi rice

2 tablespoons of rice vinegar

2 tablespoons of sugar

1 teaspoon of salt

8 oz of cooked crab meat

1 small cucumber, peeled and sliced into thin strips

1 tablespoon of mayonnaise (low FODMAP)

1 tablespoon of gluten-free soy sauce

1 teaspoon of wasabi (optional)

Pickled ginger (optional)

INSTRUCTIONS:

Cook the sushi rice in accordance with the instructions provided on the box, and then let it to cool to room temperature.

Rice vinegar, sugar, and salt should all be combined in a small bowl and stirred together until the sugar and salt have dissolved.

Once the sushi rice has cooled, add the vinegar mixture and toss it together until it is completely incorporated.

Place a sheet of nori seaweed with the glossy side facing down on a sushi rolling mat.

On top of the nori seaweed, spread a thin layer of rice, being sure to leave a border of about 1 inch at the top edge.

On top of the rice, arrange a strip of crab meat and several slices of cucumber.

Tightly roll the sushi using the mat as a guide so that it has the proper form.

Proceed with the remaining Components in the same manner.

Use a sharp knife to slice the sushi rolls into pieces that are suitable for eating immediately.

Mayonnaise, wasabi, gluten-free soy sauce, and pickled ginger should be served with the dish (if desired).

CALORIES AND MACROS PER SERVING:

Calories: 328

Carbs: 60g

Protein: 12g

Fat: 3g

STEAK SALAD WITH LOW FODMAP VEGGIES

SERVINGS: 2

PREPARATION TIME: 20 minutes

INGREDIENTS:

8 oz. sirloin steak

2 cups mixed salad greens

1 cup cherry tomatoes, halved

1/2 cup sliced cucumber

1/4 cup crumbled feta cheese

1 tbsp. chopped fresh parsley

2 tbsp. olive oil

1 tbsp. red wine vinegar

Salt and pepper, to taste

INSTRUCTIONS:

Prepare a grill or grill pan by heating it to a high temperature.

Add some salt and pepper to the steak, and then cook it.

To achieve a medium-rare doneness, grill the steak for three to four minutes each side.

Before slicing the steak thinly, let it a rest for five minutes first.

Mix the olive oil, vinegar from the red wine, a pinch each of salt and pepper, and a pinch of salt in a large bowl using a whisk.

Put the salad greens, cherry tomatoes, cucumber slices, and chopped parsley in the bowl. Mix everything together.

Mix the salad with the dressing so that it is evenly coated.

Place half of the salad on each of the dishes.

Place a few slices of sliced steak and some crumbled feta cheese on top of each salad.

Immediately serve after cooking.

CALORIE AND MACRO (CARBS, PROT, FAT):

Calories: 365

Carbohydrates: 7g

Protein: 28g

Fat: 25g

BAKED SWEET POTATO WITH LOW FODMAP TOPPINGS

SERVINGS: 2

PREPARATION TIME: 10 minutes

INGREDIENTS:

2 medium sweet potatoes

1 tbsp olive oil

Salt and pepper to taste

1/2 cup lactose-free sour cream

2 green onions, green parts only, thinly sliced

1/4 cup chopped fresh parsley

1/4 cup chopped fresh chives

INSTRUCTIONS:

Turn the temperature on the oven to 400 degrees Fahrenheit (200 degrees Celsius).

Once they have been washed and pricked with a fork a few times, the sweet potatoes are ready to be baked.

Olive oil should be rubbed into the sweet potatoes, and then they should be seasoned with salt and pepper.

Bake for 45-50 minutes, or until tender.

Combine the sour cream that does not contain lactose, the green onions, the parsley, and the chives in a small bowl.

Once the sweet potatoes have been cooked through, slit them open and place a spoonful of the sour cream mixture into each one.

To be served hot.

CALORIE AND MACRO (CARBS, PROT, FAT):

Per serving:

Calories: 304

Carbs: 49g

Protein: 4g Fat: 11g

GREEK SALAD WITH LOW FODMAP VEGETABLES AND FETA CHEESE

SERVINGS: 2

PREPARATION TIME: 15 minutes

INGREDIENTS:

4 cups mixed salad greens

1 cup chopped low FODMAP vegetables (cucumber, bell peppers, tomatoes)

1/2 cup crumbled feta cheese

2 tbsp chopped fresh parsley

2 tbsp olive oil

1 tbsp lemon juice

1/2 tsp dried oregano

Salt and pepper to taste

INSTRUCTIONS:

To make the salad, combine the salad greens, veggies that have been chopped, feta cheese, and fresh parsley in a big bowl.

Olive oil, fresh lemon juice, dried oregano, salt, and pepper should be mixed together in a small basin using a whisk.

After pouring the dressing over the salad, toss it to evenly cover the ingredients.

Serve right away, and have fun with it!

CALORIE AND MACRO (CARBS, PROT, FAT):

Calories: 265

Carbohydrates: 11g

Protein: 8g

Fat: 22g

CHICKEN AND VEGETABLE KEBABS WITH QUINOA

SERVINGS: 4

PREPARATION TIME: 25 minutes

INGREDIENTS:

1 lb boneless, skinless chicken breasts, cut into cubes

2 bell peppers, cut into chunks

1 zucchini, cut into chunks

1 yellow squash, cut into chunks

1/4 cup olive oil

1 tbsp. garlic-infused oil

1 tbsp. fresh lemon juice

1 tsp. dried oregano

1/2 tsp. salt

1/4 tsp. black pepper

1 cup cooked quinoa

INSTRUCTIONS:

Prepare the grill for cooking over medium-high heat.

Mix together olive oil, oil that has been infused with garlic, lemon juice, oregano, salt, and black pepper in a small bowl using a whisk.

Skewers should be loaded with chicken, red and green bell peppers, zucchini, and yellow squash.

Coat the skewers with the olive oil and garlic mixture and set aside.

Cook the skewers over a grill for ten to twelve minutes, turning them every so often, until the chicken is completely cooked through and the veggies are soft.

Serve on quinoa that has been cooked.

CALORIE AND MACRO (CARBS, PROT, FAT):

Per serving: 387 calories, 27g protein, 25g carbohydrates, 19g fat

LOW FODMAP CHICKEN AND VEGETABLE STIR-FRY WITH RICE NOODLES

SERVINGS: 4

PREPARATION TIME: 20 minutes

INGREDIENTS:

8 oz. low FODMAP rice noodles

2 tbsp. olive oil

1 lb. boneless, skinless chicken breast, cut into thin strips

1 red bell pepper, sliced

1 yellow bell pepper, sliced

1 zucchini, sliced

1 cup snow peas

2 tbsp. low FODMAP soy sauce

2 tbsp. oyster sauce

1 tsp. garlic-infused oil

1 tsp. grated fresh ginger

Salt and pepper to taste

Sesame seeds for garnish

INSTRUCTIONS:

Rice noodles should be prepared in accordance with the instructions provided on the box. Drain, then put to the side.

Olive oil should be heated up over high heat in a wok or a big pan.

Stir-fry the chicken for three to four minutes, or until it is completely cooked through.

Stir fry the bell peppers, zucchini, and snow peas for two to three minutes, or until the veggies reach a crisp-tender consistency, whichever comes first.

In a pan over medium heat, combine cooked rice noodles, oyster sauce, soy sauce, oil infused with garlic, grated ginger, and a pinch each of salt and pepper. Cook for a further one to two minutes after giving everything a good toss.

To serve, bring to a boil and sprinkle with toasted sesame seeds.

CALORIE AND MACRO (CARBS, PROT, FAT):

Calories: 398

Carbohydrates: 52g Protein: 28g Fat: 9g

GRILLED SHRIMP WITH QUINOA SALAD

SERVINGS: 4

PREPARATION TIME: 20 minutes

COOK TIME: 15 minutes

INGREDIENTS:

For the Shrimp:

1 pound large shrimp, peeled and deveined

1 tablespoon olive oil

2 garlic cloves, minced

1 teaspoon paprika

Salt and pepper, to taste

4 skewers

For the Quinoa Salad:

1 cup quinoa

2 cups water

1/2 teaspoon salt

1 red bell pepper, chopped

1 yellow bell pepper, chopped

1/2 cup chopped red onion

1/2 cup chopped fresh parsley

1/4 cup chopped fresh mint

1/4 cup olive oil

2 tablespoons lemon juice

Salt and pepper, to taste

INSTRUCTIONS:

Prepare the grill for cooking over medium-high heat.

Toss the shrimp with some olive oil, garlic, paprika, salt, and pepper before placing them in a medium bowl. Skewer the shrimp using thread or skewers.

Put the shrimp skewers on the grill and cook for about three to four minutes on each side, or until the shrimp become pink and are fully cooked.

While the shrimp are boiling, drain the quinoa in a colander with a fine mesh and run it under cold water. Place the quinoa, water, and salt in a pot of medium size, and then bring the mixture to a boil over high heat. After 15–20 minutes, or until the water is absorbed and the quinoa is cooked, reduce the heat to low, cover, and simmer the mixture.

Mix together the cooked quinoa, the red bell pepper, the yellow bell pepper, the red onion, the parsley, and the mint in a large bowl.

Olive oil, lemon juice, salt, and pepper should be mixed together in a small basin using a whisk. When the dressing has been drizzled over the quinoa salad, give it a good spin to cover everything.

As a side dish to the quinoa salad, serve the grilled shrimp.

CALORIE AND MACRO (CARBS, PROT, FAT):

Calories per serving: 377

Carbohydrates: 28g

Protein: 27g

Fat: 17g

LOW FODMAP CHICKEN CAESAR SALAD

SERVINGS:4

PREPARATION TIME: 15 minutes

INGREDIENTS:

1 lb boneless, skinless chicken breasts

1 head of romaine lettuce, chopped

1/2 cup cherry tomatoes, halved

1/2 cup cucumber, sliced

1/4 cup grated Parmesan cheese

1/4 cup low FODMAP Caesar dressing

Salt and pepper to taste

INSTRUCTIONS:

Turn the oven up to 400 degrees Fahrenheit.

Add some salt and pepper to the chicken breasts, then place them in the oven for 20 to 25 minutes, or until the chicken is completely cooked.

While the chicken is in the oven, you may cut the lettuce and cucumber into thin slices and cut the cherry tomatoes in half.

Combine the Caesar dressing and the Parmesan cheese in a small bowl and whisk until smooth.

Wait five minutes after the chicken has finished cooking before slicing it once you have given it time to rest.

Combine the chopped lettuce, sliced cucumber, and half cherry tomatoes in a large bowl and toss to combine.

Place the cut chicken in the bowl, then pour the Caesar dressing mixture over the chicken. Serve immediately.

Mix everything together until the salad is completely covered in the dressing and the ingredients are uniformly distributed.

Serve, and have fun with it!

CALORIES AND MACROS (CARBS, PROTEIN, FAT)

Per serving (1/4 of recipe):

Calories: 200

Carbohydrates: 6g

Protein: 26g

Fat: 8g

GRILLED SALMON WITH ROASTED VEGETABLES

4 SERVINGS

PREPARATION TIME: 30 minutes

Cook time: 20 minutes

INGREDIENTS:

4 salmon fillets (4-6 oz each)

2 cups broccoli florets

2 cups sliced zucchini

2 cups sliced bell peppers

1/4 cup olive oil

2 tbsp lemon juice

1 tsp dried basil

1 tsp dried oregano

Salt and pepper to taste

INSTRUCTIONS:

Turn the temperature on the oven to 400 degrees Fahrenheit (200 degrees Celsius).

Olive oil, lemon juice, dried basil, dried oregano, salt, and pepper are mixed together in a bowl with olive oil.

Place the broccoli florets, sliced zucchini, and sliced bell peppers in a separate dish. Use half of the olive oil mixture to toss the vegetables.

Place the veggies in an even layer on a baking sheet, then roast in the oven for about 20 minutes, or until the vegetables are soft.

In the meanwhile, bring the grill to a medium-high temperature.

Use a pastry brush to apply the remaining olive oil mixture on the salmon fillets.

Grill the salmon for 4-5 minutes each side, or until cooked through.

Serve the grilled fish with the roasted veggies.

Calories and macro (carbs, protein, fat):

Calories: 392

Carbs: 10g

Protein: 35g

Fat: 24g

LOW FODMAP CHICKEN AND VEGETABLE SKEWERS WITH QUINOA

SERVINGS: 4

PREPARATION TIME: 30 minutes

INGREDIENTS

For the skewers:

1 lb boneless, skinless chicken breasts, cut into 1-inch pieces

2 red bell peppers, seeded and cut into 1-inch pieces

2 zucchinis, sliced into rounds

1 tablespoon garlic-infused olive oil

1/2 teaspoon dried oregano

Salt and pepper, to taste

Wooden skewers, soaked in water for 30 minutes

For the quinoa:

1 cup quinoa, rinsed and drained

2 cups water

1/4 teaspoon salt

For the dressing:

1/4 cup freshly squeezed lemon juice

1/4 cup extra-virgin olive oil

1 tablespoon Dijon mustard

1 tablespoon honey

Salt and pepper, to taste

INSTRUCTIONS

Prepare the grill by heating it to a medium-high temperature.

Mix the chicken, bell peppers, zucchini, garlic-infused olive oil, oregano, and salt and pepper together in a large bowl. Mix everything together until the chicken and veggies are uniformly covered.

Skewer the chicken and veggies, rotating between each one as you go, using the skewers.

Cook the kebabs on the grill for 12 to 15 minutes, flipping them every so often, until the chicken is completely cooked through and the veggies are soft.

Prepare the quinoa while the skewers are in the grilling process. The quinoa, water, and salt should be brought to a boil in a pot of medium size. Turn the heat down to low, cover the pot, and let it simmer for 15 to 20 minutes, or until the quinoa is cooked through and all of the water has been absorbed.

To prepare the dressing, take a small bowl and mix together the lemon juice, olive oil, Dijon mustard, honey, and seasonings of your choice (salt and pepper).

The skewers should be served with quinoa, and the dressing should be brought on the side.

CALORIE AND MACRO (CARBS, PROT, FAT)

Per serving:

Calories: 350

Carbohydrates: 30g

Protein: 26g

Fat: 14g

TURKEY LETTUCE WRAPS WITH LOW FODMAP DIPPING SAUCE

SERVINGS: 4

PREPARATION TIME: 30 minutes

INGREDIENTS:

For the lettuce wraps:

1 pound ground turkey

1 tablespoon olive oil

1 tablespoon garlic-infused oil

2 tablespoons low FODMAP soy sauce

1 teaspoon ground ginger

1 teaspoon rice vinegar

1/4 teaspoon black pepper

1/4 teaspoon salt

8 large lettuce leaves, such as Bibb or butter lettuce

1/4 cup shredded carrots

1/4 cup chopped scallions (green parts only)

1/4 cup chopped cilantro

1/4 cup chopped peanuts

For the low FODMAP dipping sauce:

2 tablespoons low FODMAP soy sauce

2 tablespoons rice vinegar

1 tablespoon maple syrup

1 tablespoon garlic-infused oil

1/4 teaspoon ground ginger

113

1/4 teaspoon red pepper flakes

INSTRUCTIONS:

Warm the olive oil and the oil that has been infused with garlic in a large pan over medium heat. After adding the ground turkey, sauté it over medium heat until it is browned, breaking it up with a wooden spoon as it cooks.

Combine the low FODMAP soy sauce, the ground ginger, the rice vinegar, the black pepper, and the salt in a small bowl and whisk to combine. After pouring the sauce over the turkey that has been cooked, toss it to blend the ingredients. Continue to cook for an additional two to three minutes.

In order to produce the dipping sauce that is low in FODMAPs, combine in a small bowl the soy sauce that is low in FODMAPs, the rice vinegar, the maple syrup, the garlic-infused oil, the ground ginger, and the red pepper flakes.

To make the lettuce wraps, just place a little of the turkey mixture on each leaf of lettuce using a spoon. Garnish with shredded carrots, sliced scallions and peanuts, chopped cilantro, and fresh cilantro. To accompany the dish, low FODMAP dipping sauce should be served on the side.

CALORIES AND MACROS:

Per serving:

Calories: 247

Carbs: 6g

Protein: 23g

Fat: 15g

GRILLED CHICKEN WITH LOW FODMAP VEGETABLES AND BROWN RICE

SERVINGS

4 SERVINGS

PREPARATION TIME

10 minutes

INGREDIENTS

4 boneless, skinless chicken breasts

1 cup low FODMAP vegetables, such as bell peppers, zucchini, and eggplant, sliced

1 tbsp. garlic-infused oil

2 tbsp. low FODMAP balsamic vinaigrette

2 cups cooked brown rice

Salt and pepper to taste

INSTRUCTIONS

Prepare the grill by heating it to a medium-high temperature.

Add salt and pepper to the chicken breasts before cooking them.

Toss the veggies in a big bowl with some garlic-infused oil, and then season them with salt and pepper to taste.

Cook the chicken on the grill for 6–8 minutes each side, or until it is fully done.

Grill the veggies for 3-4 minutes each side or until tender.

Blend the balsamic vinaigrette ingredients together in a small bowl using a whisk.

Brown rice that has been cooked should be served as the base for the chicken and veggies that have been grilled, and the balsamic vinaigrette should be drizzled on top.

CALORIE AND MACRO (CARBS, PROT, FAT)

Calories per serving: 356

Carbohydrates: 39g

Protein: 32g

Fat: 8g

LOW FODMAP TUNA AND AVOCADO SALAD

SERVINGS

2 SERVINGS

PREPARATION TIME

10 minutes

INGREDIENTS

1 can of tuna, drained

1 small avocado, diced

1/4 cup of chopped celery

1/4 cup of chopped red bell pepper

2 tbsp of chopped fresh parsley

2 tbsp of mayonnaise

1 tbsp of lemon juice

Salt and pepper to taste

INSTRUCTIONS

In a medium bowl, combine the tuna, avocado, celery, red bell pepper, and parsley.

In a small bowl, whisk together the mayonnaise and lemon juice until smooth.

Pour the mayonnaise mixture over the tuna and avocado mixture and stir until evenly coated.

Season with salt and pepper to taste.

Serve the tuna and avocado salad on a bed of lettuce leaves, if desired.

CALORIE AND MACRO (CARBS, PROT, FAT)

Per serving:

Calories: 253

Carbs: 8g

Protein: 17g

Fat: 18g

CHICKEN AND VEGETABLE KABOBS WITH BROWN RICE

4 SERVINGS

PREPARATION TIME: 30 minutes

Cook time: 20 minutes

INGREDIENTS:

2 chicken breasts, cut into 1-inch cubes

1 red bell pepper, cut into 1-inch pieces

1 yellow bell pepper, cut into 1-inch pieces

1 zucchini, cut into 1/2-inch rounds

1/4 cup olive oil

1/4 cup low-sodium soy sauce

2 tablespoons honey

2 tablespoons minced fresh ginger

1 tablespoon minced garlic

1 tablespoon sesame oil

Salt and pepper, to taste

2 cups cooked brown rice

INSTRUCTIONS:

Preheat grill to medium-high heat.

In a large bowl, whisk together olive oil, soy sauce, honey, ginger, garlic, sesame oil, salt, and pepper. Reserve 1/4 cup of the mixture for basting later.

Add chicken, bell peppers, and zucchini to the bowl with the marinade. Toss to coat and let sit for 10-15 minutes.

Thread the chicken and vegetables onto skewers, alternating between the chicken and veggies.

Grill the skewers for 8-10 minutes per side, basting with the reserved marinade every few minutes.

Serve the kabobs with brown rice.

Calories and Macro (carbs, prot, fat):

Calories: 360

Carbs: 45g

Protein: 28g

Fat: 9g

BAKED SWEET POTATO WITH LOW FODMAP TUNA SALAD

2 SERVINGS

PREPARATION TIME: 10 minutes

Cook time: 45 minutes

INGREDIENTS:

2 medium sweet potatoes

1 can of tuna in water, drained

1/4 cup of mayonnaise (low FODMAP, if needed)

1 tablespoon of Dijon mustard

2 tablespoons of chopped chives

Salt and pepper to taste

INSTRUCTIONS:

Preheat the oven to 400°F (200°C).

Scrub the sweet potatoes and pierce them a few times with a fork.

Place the sweet potatoes on a baking sheet lined with parchment paper and bake for 45 minutes, or until they are tender.

While the sweet potatoes are baking, prepare the tuna salad. In a small mixing bowl, mix together the drained tuna, mayonnaise, Dijon mustard, chopped chives, salt, and pepper.

Once the sweet potatoes are done, remove them from the oven and let them cool for a few minutes.

Cut open the sweet potatoes and top them with the tuna salad mixture.

Serve and enjoy!

Calorie and Macro (carbs, protein, fat):

Per serving:

Calories: 344

Carbs: 35g

Protein: 13g

Fat: 16g

GRILLED SHRIMP AND VEGETABLE SKEWERS WITH QUINOA SALAD

SERVINGS: 4

PREPARATION TIME: 30 minutes

INGREDIENTS:

1 lb large shrimp, peeled and deveined

2 red bell peppers, cut into 1-inch pieces

1 zucchini, sliced into 1/4-inch rounds

1 red onion, cut into 1-inch pieces

1/4 cup olive oil

2 cloves garlic, minced

2 tablespoons lemon juice

1/2 teaspoon dried oregano

1/2 teaspoon dried thyme

1/2 teaspoon salt

1/4 teaspoon black pepper

2 cups cooked quinoa

1 cup grape tomatoes, halved

1/4 cup chopped fresh parsley

1/4 cup chopped fresh mint

1/4 cup crumbled feta cheese

INSTRUCTIONS:

Preheat grill to medium-high heat.

Thread shrimp, bell peppers, zucchini, and red onion onto skewers, alternating between each ingredient.

In a small bowl, whisk together olive oil, garlic, lemon juice, oregano, thyme, salt, and black pepper.

Brush the skewers with the olive oil mixture.

Grill skewers for 3-4 minutes per side, or until the shrimp is pink and cooked through.

In a large bowl, combine cooked quinoa, grape tomatoes, parsley, mint, and feta cheese.

Serve grilled shrimp and vegetable skewers with quinoa salad.

CALORIE AND MACRO (CARBS, PROT, FAT):

Calories: 392

Carbohydrates: 30g

Protein: 29g

Fat: 17g

LOW FODMAP CHICKEN AND VEGETABLE STIR-FRY WITH QUINOA

SERVINGS: 4

PREPARATION TIME: 30 minutes

INGREDIENTS:

1 cup quinoa

2 cups water

2 tablespoons olive oil

2 boneless, skinless chicken breasts, sliced into strips

1 red bell pepper, sliced

1 yellow bell pepper, sliced

1 small zucchini, sliced

2 tablespoons low FODMAP soy sauce

1 tablespoon grated fresh ginger

2 tablespoons chopped green onion (green part only)

Salt and pepper, to taste

INSTRUCTIONS:

Rinse the quinoa in a fine mesh strainer and place it in a pot with 2 cups of water. Bring to a boil, reduce heat, and simmer for 15-20 minutes, until the water is absorbed and the quinoa is tender. Fluff with a fork and set aside.

Heat 1 tablespoon of olive oil in a large skillet over medium-high heat. Add the chicken and cook for 5-7 minutes, until browned and cooked through. Remove the chicken from the skillet and set aside.

Add the remaining tablespoon of olive oil to the skillet. Add the bell peppers and zucchini and cook for 5-7 minutes, until the vegetables are tender-crisp.

Return the chicken to the skillet with the vegetables. Add the low FODMAP soy sauce, grated ginger, and chopped green onion. Stir to combine and cook for 2-3 minutes, until everything is heated through.

Divide the quinoa among four plates and top each with a portion of the chicken and vegetable stir-fry. Season with salt and pepper, if desired.

CALORIE AND MACRO (CARBS, PROT, FAT):

Calories: 326

Carbs: 35g

Protein: 26g

Fat: 9g

TURKEY AND CHEESE LETTUCE WRAPS WITH LOW FODMAP TOPPINGS

SERVINGS: 4

PREPARATION TIME: 15 minutes

INGREDIENTS:

1 pound ground turkey

1 teaspoon garlic-infused oil

1/2 teaspoon ground cumin

1/2 teaspoon paprika

Salt and pepper to taste

8 large lettuce leaves

4 slices cheddar cheese

Low FODMAP toppings of your choice (such as sliced tomatoes, sliced cucumber, sliced bell peppers, sliced olives, etc.)

INSTRUCTIONS:

In a large pan set over medium heat, warm the oil that has been flavored with garlic.

After adding the ground turkey, continue cooking it until it has a browned appearance, while breaking it up into little pieces as it cooks.

To the pan, add the paprika, cumin, salt, and pepper, and mix to blend all of the ingredients.

Cook the turkey for a another hour or so, or until it is no longer pink in the center.

To put together the lettuce wraps, start by placing a piece of cheese on each individual lettuce leaf.

The cooked turkey should be distributed equally among the lettuce leaves.

You may fill each lettuce wrap with any low FODMAP toppings you like most.

To make a wrap out of the lettuce leaves, roll them up.

Immediately serve after cooking.

CALORIE AND MACRO (CARBS, PROT, FAT)

Calories: 267

Carbs: 5g

Protein: 31g

Fat: 13g

DINNER

1. Grilled pork tenderloin with roasted carrots and parsnips

2. Low FODMAP zucchini and tomato quiche

3. Lemon herb roasted chicken with green beans

4. Low FODMAP beef and broccoli stir-fry with rice noodles

5. Garlic roasted shrimp with asparagus and brown rice

6. Low FODMAP eggplant parmesan with mixed greens salad

7. Pan-seared scallops with roasted brussels sprouts and sweet potato mash

8. Low FODMAP stuffed bell peppers with ground turkey and quinoa

9. Herb marinated lamb chops with grilled eggplant and red pepper

10. Low FODMAP spaghetti squash with turkey meatballs and tomato sauce

11. Cilantro lime grilled fish with roasted cauliflower and quinoa

GRILLED PORK TENDERLOIN WITH ROASTED CARROTS AND PARSNIPS

SERVINGS: 4

PREPARATION TIME: 1 hour

INGREDIENTS:

1 pound pork tenderloin

1 teaspoon garlic powder

1 teaspoon onion powder

1 teaspoon smoked paprika

1/2 teaspoon salt

1/4 teaspoon black pepper

1 tablespoon olive oil

1 pound carrots, peeled and sliced into sticks

1 pound parsnips, peeled and sliced into sticks

2 tablespoons olive oil

Salt and pepper to taste

INSTRUCTIONS:

Lightly oil the grill grates and set the grill to medium-high heat.

Garlic powder, onion powder, smoked paprika, salt, and black pepper should be combined in a small bowl.

Use the spice blend to coat the pork tenderloin.

One tablespoon of olive oil should be drizzled over the pork tenderloin.

Cook the pork tenderloin on the grill for 20 to 25 minutes, or until an instant-read thermometer registers 145 degrees Fahrenheit.

After 5-10 minutes resting time, take the pork tenderloin off the grill and slice it into 1/2-inch-thick slices.

Turn the oven temperature up to 400 degrees Fahrenheit.

Combine the carrots and parsnips with 2 tablespoons of olive oil in a large bowl.

Put in as much salt and pepper as you want.

Put the veggies on a baking sheet in a single layer.

Cook the veggies in the oven for 20 to 25 minutes, or until they reach the desired tenderness and colour.

Toss the roasted carrots and parsnips with the sliced pork tenderloin and serve.

Calories: 335 | Carbohydrates: 20g | Protein: 29g | Fat: 16g

LOW FODMAP ZUCCHINI AND TOMATO QUICHE

SERVINGS: 6

PREPARATION TIME: 15 minutes

INGREDIENTS:

1 pre-made gluten-free pie crust

2 tbsp. olive oil

2 small zucchinis, sliced

2 small tomatoes, sliced

4 large eggs

1 cup lactose-free milk

1/4 cup chopped fresh basil

Salt and pepper to taste

1 cup shredded lactose-free cheese

INSTRUCTIONS:

Get ready an oven preheated to 375 degrees Fahrenheit (190 degrees Celsius).

Olive oil should be heated in a pan over medium heat.

Sliced zucchinis should be added and cooked for 5 minutes, or until they are just soft.

Combine the eggs, lactose-free milk, basil, salt, and pepper in a bowl and whisk together.

Make use of a 9-inch pie plate to house the prepared pie dough.

Layer the pie crust with the cut tomatoes and zucchini.

Sprinkle the veggies with the egg mixture.

Shredded lactose-free cheese makes a delicious topping for the quiche.

For about 35-40 minutes in a preheated oven, or until the filling has set and the top is golden, bake the quiche.

You should wait a few minutes for the quiche to cool before cutting it.

Calorie and Macro (Carbs, Prot, Fat):

Calories: 340

Carbohydrates: 22g

Protein: 13g

Fat: 23g

LEMON HERB ROASTED CHICKEN WITH GREEN BEANS

SERVINGS: 4

PREPARATION TIME: 10 minutes

Cook Time: 50 minutes

INGREDIENTS:

4 chicken breasts, bone-in and skin-on

1 lb fresh green beans, trimmed

3 tbsp olive oil

2 lemons, sliced

4 cloves garlic, minced

2 tbsp fresh rosemary, finely chopped

2 tbsp fresh thyme, finely chopped

1 tsp salt

1/2 tsp black pepper

INSTRUCTIONS:

Turn the oven temperature up to 400 degrees Fahrenheit (200 degrees Celsius).

Olive oil, garlic, rosemary, thyme, salt, and pepper should all be mixed together in a big bowl. Toss everything together.

Place the chicken breasts in the bowl and toss them around so that they are well covered in the herb mixture.

Spread the chicken breasts, skin side up, on a baking sheet. Cover the chicken with the lemon slices.

Prepare an oven to 400 degrees and roast the chicken for 40 minutes.

After 40 minutes, combine the chicken breasts with the pan juices and add the green beans, which have been trimmed.

After the chicken is fully done and the green beans are soft but still crisp, place the baking sheet back in the oven and roast for another 10 to 12 minutes.

After the timer goes off, take the chicken and green beans out of the oven and let them rest for 5 minutes before serving.

CALORIE AND MACRO (CARBS, PROT, FAT):

Calories: 450

Carbs: 12g

Protein: 50g

Fat: 22g

LOW FODMAP BEEF AND BROCCOLI STIR-FRY WITH RICE NOODLES

SERVINGS: 4

PREPARATION TIME: 30 minutes

INGREDIENTS:

8 oz. rice noodles

1 lb. flank steak, thinly sliced

3 tbsp. low FODMAP soy sauce

2 tbsp. rice vinegar

2 tbsp. maple syrup

2 tbsp. sesame oil

1 tbsp. cornstarch

1 tbsp. grated ginger

2 cloves garlic, minced

1 head broccoli, chopped

1 red bell pepper, sliced

2 tbsp. chopped scallions, for garnish

INSTRUCTIONS:

Noodles should be prepared in accordance with the package's directions and then put aside.

Blend the sauce ingredients (soy sauce, rice vinegar, maple syrup, sesame oil, cornstarch, ginger, and garlic) in a small bowl.

A good amount of oil should be heated over high heat in a big pan or wok. Slice the steak and cook it for about two minutes on each side, or until it is browned.

After about 2 to 3 minutes, or until the broccoli and bell pepper are just beginning to soften, add the veggies to the pan.

After the sauce has thickened and the veggies are covered, pour it into the pan and give everything a good swirl.

Lastly, throw in the cooked rice noodles and serve.

Serve immediately while still hot, and top with sliced scallions.

CALORIES AND MACROS PER SERVING:

Calories: 475

Carbs: 52g

Protein: 28g

Fat: 18g

GARLIC ROASTED SHRIMP WITH ASPARAGUS AND BROWN RICE

SERVINGS: 4

PREPARATION TIME: 30 minutes

INGREDIENTS:

1 lb large shrimp, peeled and deveined

1 lb asparagus, trimmed and cut into 2-inch pieces

4 garlic cloves, minced

2 tbsp olive oil and salt and pepper

2 cups cooked brown rice

INSTRUCTIONS:

Turn the oven temperature up to 400 degrees Fahrenheit.

Toss the shrimp and asparagus with the olive oil and chopped garlic in a large basin until everything is well covered.

Add pepper and salt to taste.

On a baking sheet, arrange the shrimp and asparagus in a single layer.

Prepare for 10-12 minutes in the oven, or until the shrimp are pink and fully cooked and the asparagus is soft.

Place the shrimp and asparagus on top of cooked brown rice and serve.

Nutrition Information (per serving):

Calories: 280

Carbohydrates: 28g

Protein: 28g

Fat: 7g

LOW FODMAP EGGPLANT PARMESAN WITH MIXED GREENS SALAD

SERVINGS: 4

PREPARATION TIME: 45 minutes

INGREDIENTS:

1 large eggplant, sliced into rounds

1/2 cup gluten-free breadcrumbs

1/4 cup grated parmesan cheese

1 egg

1/2 cup low FODMAP marinara sauce

1/2 cup shredded mozzarella cheese

4 cups mixed greens

1/4 cup sliced cherry tomatoes

1/4 cup sliced cucumber

2 tbsp balsamic vinaigrette

Salt and pepper to taste

Olive oil cooking spray

INSTRUCTIONS:

Get ready an oven preheated to 375 degrees Fahrenheit (190 degrees Celsius).

Place the gluten-free breadcrumbs and grated parmesan cheese in a pie plate or other shallow dish and mix well. The egg should be beaten in another bowl.

Battered egg is used to coat the eggplant rounds before they are dipped in the breadcrumb mixture.

Spray a baking sheet with olive oil cooking spray and arrange the eggplant rounds on it.

For about 20 minutes, or until they reach the desired crispiness and light browning in the oven, bake the eggplant circles.

After baking, remove the eggplant rounds and top each with some shredded mozzarella and low FODMAP marinara sauce.

For a further 10 to 15 minutes, or until the cheese is melted and bubbling, return the eggplant rounds to the oven.

A salad of mixed greens, cherry tomatoes, and cucumber may be tossed together in a dish while the eggplant bakes. Season the salad with salt and pepper to taste, then drizzle over some balsamic vinaigrette.

The eggplant parmesan and the greens salad make a great meal.

Calories per serving: 240

Carbs: 23g | Protein: 11g | Fat: 11g

PAN-SEARED SCALLOPS WITH ROASTED BRUSSELS SPROUTS AND SWEET POTATO MASH

SERVINGS: 2

PREPARATION TIME: 30 minutes

INGREDIENTS:

6 large scallops, cleaned and patted dry

1/2 lb Brussels sprouts, trimmed and halved

1 medium-sized sweet potato, peeled and cubed

2 tablespoons olive oil, divided

1/2 teaspoon dried thyme

Salt and pepper to taste

INSTRUCTIONS:

Turn the oven temperature up to 400F (200C).

Stir the Brussels sprouts, thyme, salt, and pepper together in a mixing dish with 1 tablespoon of olive oil. Roast them for 20-25 minutes, until they are soft and beginning to color.

Boil the sweet potato until it is soft in a medium saucepan, then drain and mash it with a fork or a potato masher. Sprinkle salt and pepper to taste.

Get a skillet hot over medium heat while the Brussels sprouts roast. Drop in the last tablespoon of olive oil.

Season the scallops with salt and pepper and then pat them dry with a paper towel.

Cook the scallops for two to three minutes on each side in a heated pan until they are golden brown and opaque in the center.

Scallops should be served on a bed of sweet potato mash and roasted Brussels sprouts.

Calories and Macros:

Calories: 341

Carbohydrates: 26g

Protein: 23g

Fat: 17g

LOW FODMAP STUFFED BELL PEPPERS WITH GROUND TURKEY AND QUINOA

SERVINGS: 4

PREPARATION TIME: 45 minutes

INGREDIENTS:

4 bell peppers

1 pound ground turkey

1 cup cooked quinoa

1 cup chopped spinach

1/2 cup diced tomatoes

1/4 cup chopped green onion (green part only)

1 tablespoon olive oil

1 teaspoon paprika

1 teaspoon cumin

Salt and pepper to taste

Optional: grated cheddar cheese for topping

INSTRUCTIONS:

Start by preheating the oven to 375 degrees Fahrenheit (190 degrees Celsius).

Remove the membranes and seeds from the bell peppers, then cut off the tops.

Olive oil should be heated over medium heat in a big skillet. Ground turkey, paprika, cumin, salt, pepper, and a dash of nutmeg should be added and cooked until browned.

Cook the diced tomatoes and chopped spinach together until the spinach has wilted.

Mix in the quinoa and the sliced green onion.

Place the stuffed bell peppers in a baking dish.

Put the dish in the oven and bake for 30 minutes with the foil on top.

Take the stuffed peppers out of the foil and cover them with shredded cheese (optional).

Return to the oven and let it there for another 5-10 minutes, or until the cheese is melted and bubbling.

Please wait a few minutes for the peppers to cool before serving.

CALORIE AND MACRO (CARBS, PROT, FAT):

Carbs: 23g

Protein: 26g

Fat: 9g

HERB MARINATED LAMB CHOPS WITH GRILLED EGGPLANT AND RED PEPPER

SERVINGS: 4

PREPARATION TIME: 30 minutes (plus 2-3 hours for marinating)

INGREDIENTS:

8 lamb chops

1 large eggplant, sliced

1 red bell pepper, sliced

2 tablespoons olive oil

2 tablespoons red wine vinegar

2 tablespoons fresh lemon juice

2 garlic cloves, minced

1 tablespoon dried oregano

1 tablespoon dried thyme

Salt and pepper, to taste

INSTRUCTIONS:

Olive oil, red wine vinegar, lemon juice, garlic, oregano, thyme, salt, and pepper should be mixed together in a small dish to form the marinade.

Marinate the lamb chops by placing them in a shallow dish and pouring the marinade over them, then flipping to coat. Wrap the dish in plastic and chill it in the fridge for at least two hours, preferably longer.

Prepare a grill with medium-high heat. Pull the lamb chops out of the marinade and throw away the liquid.

Cook the lamb chops on the grill for three to four minutes each side, or until they achieve the doneness you choose.

Rub the eggplant and red pepper slices with olive oil and season with salt and pepper while the lamb chops are roasting. Cook the veggies on the grill for about three minutes each side, or until they reach the desired tenderness and charred flavor.

Roasted eggplant and red peppers are perfect accompaniments to grilled lamb chops.

Calories and Macro (carbs, prot, fat):

Calories: 460

LOW FODMAP SPAGHETTI SQUASH WITH TURKEY MEATBALLS AND TOMATO SAUCE

SERVINGS: 4

PREPARATION TIME: 45 minutes

INGREDIENTS:

1 medium spaghetti squash

1 pound ground turkey

1/2 cup gluten-free breadcrumbs

1 egg

2 tablespoons chopped fresh parsley

1 teaspoon dried oregano

1/2 teaspoon garlic powder

1/4 teaspoon salt

1/4 teaspoon black pepper

1 tablespoon olive oil

1/2 cup low FODMAP tomato sauce

Fresh basil, for garnish

INSTRUCTIONS:

Get ready an oven preheated to 375 degrees Fahrenheit (190 degrees Celsius).

The spaghetti squash has to be halved longitudinally and the seeds scraped out.

The spaghetti squash should be baked for 30 to 40 minutes with the sliced side down until soft.

Mix the turkey, breadcrumbs, egg, herbs (parsley, oregano, garlic powder, salt, and pepper), and seasonings (in a big bowl). The ingredients must be well blended, therefore mixing is required.

Make meatballs with a diameter of approximately 1 1/2 inches from the mixture.

The olive oil should be heated in a large pan over medium heat. It should take around 5 minutes to brown the meatballs on both sides after adding them to the pan.

Cooking the meatballs in the tomato sauce is a great way to ensure that they are well covered with sauce. Simmer, covered, for 10–15 minutes, or until meatballs are done.

Put the strands of spaghetti squash into a serving dish by scraping them with a fork.

Turkey meatballs and tomato sauce go well on spaghetti squash.

To serve, sprinkle with chopped fresh basil.

CALORIE AND MACRO (CARBS, PROT, FAT):

Carbs: 19g

Protein: 29g

Fat: 10g

CILANTRO LIME GRILLED FISH WITH ROASTED CAULIFLOWER AND QUINOA

SERVINGS: 4

PREPARATION TIME: 30 minutes

INGREDIENTS:

4 tilapia fillets

1/4 cup fresh lime juice

2 tablespoons olive oil

2 cloves garlic, minced

1/4 cup chopped fresh cilantro

Salt and pepper, to taste

1 head cauliflower, cut into florets

2 tablespoons olive oil

Salt and pepper, to taste

1 cup quinoa, rinsed

2 cups water

INSTRUCTIONS:

Prepare a grill with medium-high heat.

Lime juice, olive oil, garlic, cilantro, salt, and pepper are combined in a small bowl and whisked together.

Put the tilapia fillets in a shallow dish and pour the lime juice mixture over the top. Let marinate for 10-15 minutes while you prepare the cauliflower.

Mix the cauliflower florets with olive oil, salt, and pepper. In a 400°F oven, roast them in a single layer for 20 to 25 minutes, tossing them about halfway through cooking, until golden brown and soft.

Meanwhile, in a medium saucepan, bring the water to a boil. The cauliflower may go from the oven to the water. Stir in the quinoa. Turn the heat down to low and cover the pot. For best results, cover and simmer for 15–20 minutes, or until all the water is absorbed and the quinoa is soft.

Cook the tilapia fillets on the grill for three to four minutes each side, or until opaque throughout.

Serve the grilled fish over a bed of quinoa with roasted cauliflower on the side.

CALORIE AND MACRO (CARBS, PROT, FAT):

Carbs: 36g

Protein: 29g

Fat: 12g

30 DAY MEAL PLAN

This meal plan is just an example to take inspiration from and make modifications.

Day 1---

Breakfast--- Omelette with spinach and feta cheese

Lunch--- Grilled chicken with roasted vegetables

Dinner--- Grilled pork tenderloin with roasted carrots and parsnips

Day 2---

Breakfast--- Scrambled eggs with tomatoes and avocado

Lunch--- Tuna salad lettuce wraps

Dinner--- Low FODMAP zucchini and tomato quiche

Day 3---

Breakfast--- Greek yogurt with low FODMAP fruits and gluten-free granola

Lunch--- Low FODMAP vegetable stir-fry with rice

Dinner--- Lemon herb roasted chicken with green beans

Day 4---

Breakfast--- Gluten-free toast with peanut butter and banana

Lunch--- Turkey and lettuce wrap

Dinner--- Low FODMAP beef and broccoli stir-fry with rice noodles

Day 5---

Breakfast--- Breakfast smoothie with low FODMAP fruits, spinach, and almond milk

Lunch--- Low FODMAP chicken and vegetable skewers

Dinner--- Garlic roasted shrimp with asparagus and brown rice

Day 6---

Breakfast--- Gluten-free oatmeal with strawberries and almond butter

Lunch--- Grilled salmon with roasted sweet potato

Dinner--- Low FODMAP eggplant parmesan with mixed greens salad

Day 7---

Breakfast--- Rice cake with tuna and cucumber

Lunch--- Low FODMAP sushi rolls with crab and cucumber

Dinner--- Pan-seared scallops with roasted brussels sprouts and sweet potato mash

Day 8---

Breakfast--- Gluten-free toast with smoked salmon and cream cheese

Lunch--- Steak salad with low FODMAP veggies

Dinner--- Low FODMAP stuffed bell peppers with ground turkey and quinoa

Day 9---

Breakfast--- Egg muffins with spinach and cheese

Lunch--- Baked sweet potato with low FODMAP toppings

Dinner--- Herb marinated lamb chops with grilled eggplant and red pepper

Day 10---

Breakfast--- Breakfast burrito with scrambled eggs, peppers, and bacon

Lunch--- Low FODMAP Greek salad with feta cheese

Dinner--- Low FODMAP spaghetti squash with turkey meatballs and tomato sauce

Day 11---

Breakfast--- Rice cakes with almond butter and blueberries

Lunch--- Chicken and vegetable kebabs with quinoa

Dinner--- Cilantro lime grilled fish with roasted cauliflower and quinoa

Day 12---

Breakfast--- Gluten-free granola with yogurt and low FODMAP fruits

Lunch--- Low FODMAP chicken and vegetable stir-fry with rice noodles

Dinner--- Grilled pork tenderloin with roasted carrots and parsnips

Day 13---

Breakfast--- Breakfast hash with sweet potatoes, peppers, and sausage

Lunch--- Turkey burger with low FODMAP toppings

Dinner--- Low FODMAP zucchini and tomato quiche

Day 14---

Breakfast--- Gluten-free pancakes with blueberries and maple syrup

Lunch--- Grilled shrimp with quinoa salad

Dinner--- Lemon herb roasted chicken with green beans

Day 15---

Breakfast--- Shakshuka with tomato, bell pepper, and eggs

Lunch--- Low FODMAP chicken Caesar salad

Dinner--- Low FODMAP beef and broccoli stir-fry with rice noodles

Day 16---

Breakfast--- Gluten-free toast with peanut butter and banana

Lunch--- Low FODMAP chicken Caesar salad

Dinner--- Lemon herb roasted chicken with green beans

Day 17---

Breakfast--- Greek yogurt with low FODMAP fruits and gluten-free granola

Lunch--- Grilled shrimp with quinoa salad

Dinner--- Low FODMAP beef and broccoli stir-fry with rice noodles

Day 18---

Breakfast--- Breakfast smoothie with low FODMAP fruits, spinach, and almond milk

Lunch--- Turkey burger with low FODMAP toppings

Dinner--- Garlic roasted shrimp with asparagus and brown rice

Day 19---

Breakfast--- Rice cakes with almond butter and blueberries

Lunch--- Grilled chicken with low FODMAP vegetables and brown rice

Dinner--- Low FODMAP eggplant parmesan with mixed greens salad

Day 20---

Breakfast--- Gluten-free granola with yogurt and low FODMAP fruits

Lunch--- Turkey and cheese lettuce wraps with low FODMAP toppings

Dinner--- Low FODMAP stuffed bell peppers with ground turkey and quinoa

Day 21---

Breakfast--- Frittata with spinach, tomatoes, and goat cheese

Lunch--- Low FODMAP chicken and vegetable stir-fry with rice noodles

Dinner--- Herb marinated lamb chops with grilled eggplant and red pepper

Day 22---

Breakfast--- Gluten-free oatmeal with raspberries and almonds

Lunch--- Baked sweet potato with low FODMAP tuna salad

Dinner--- Low FODMAP spaghetti squash with turkey meatballs and tomato sauce

Day 23---

Breakfast--- Rice cake with tuna and cucumber

Lunch--- Grilled shrimp and vegetable skewers with quinoa salad

Dinner--- Cilantro lime grilled fish with roasted cauliflower and quinoa

Day 24---

Breakfast--- Breakfast burrito with black beans, scrambled eggs, and cheese

Lunch--- Low FODMAP chicken and vegetable skewers with quinoa

Dinner--- Grilled pork tenderloin with roasted carrots and parsnips

Day 25---

Breakfast--- Gluten-free toast with smoked salmon and cream cheese

Lunch--- Turkey lettuce wraps with low FODMAP dipping sauce

Dinner--- Low FODMAP zucchini and tomato quiche

Day 26---

Breakfast--- Chia seed pudding with low FODMAP fruits and coconut milk

Lunch--- Low FODMAP Greek salad with feta cheese

Dinner--- Pan-seared scallops with roasted brussels sprouts and sweet potato mash

Day 27---

Breakfast--- Breakfast bowl with quinoa, scrambled eggs, and avocado

Lunch--- Chicken and vegetable kebabs with quinoa

Dinner--- Low FODMAP beef and broccoli stir-fry with rice noodles

Day 28---

Breakfast--- Gluten-free waffles with strawberries and whipped cream

Lunch--- Grilled chicken with roasted vegetables

Dinner--- Low FODMAP stuffed bell peppers with ground turkey and quinoa

Day 29---

Breakfast--- Breakfast sandwich with gluten-free bread, egg, and ham

Lunch--- Low FODMAP chicken Caesar salad

Dinner--- Lemon herb roasted chicken with green beans

Day 30---

Breakfast--- Omelette with spinach and feta cheese

Lunch--- Low FODMAP tuna and avocado salad

Dinner--- Cilantro lime grilled fish with roasted cauliflower and quinoa

CONCLUSION

Throughout the pages of this book, we have explored the intricacies of inflammation and its impact on our overall health and wellbeing. From the role of the gut microbiome to the importance of maintaining a balanced diet, we have uncovered a wealth of knowledge and practical tools for managing inflammation through food. Specifically, we have focused on the FODMAP diet, a dietary approach that has been shown to have anti-inflammatory properties and is particularly beneficial for those suffering from IBS.

The FODMAP diet emphasizes the importance of limiting certain types of carbohydrates that can be difficult to digest and may exacerbate inflammation. By following the guidelines of the FODMAP diet, individuals can manage their IBS symptoms and reduce inflammation, leading to improved digestive health and overall wellness. And with the wide range of delicious and nutritious recipes included in this book, readers can discover how to make the FODMAP diet an enjoyable and sustainable part of their daily routine.

By taking a proactive approach to our health and wellbeing, we can achieve greater control over our lives and improve our quality of life. With the knowledge and tools provided in this book, readers can embark on a journey towards better health and happiness, one meal at a time. Whether you are struggling with IBS or simply seeking to adopt a healthier lifestyle, the principles of an anti-inflammatory diet and the FODMAP approach can help you achieve your goals and thrive in all areas of your life.

INDEX

BONUS HIIT

High-intensity interval training (HIIT) is a popular form of exercise that involves short bursts of intense exercise followed by periods of rest or lower intensity exercise. HIIT workouts typically last between 20-30 minutes and can provide numerous health benefits, including improved cardiovascular fitness, increased muscle strength, and enhanced fat loss.

The intensity of HIIT exercises is what sets them apart from other forms of cardio exercise. During the high-intensity intervals, you push your body to its maximum effort, which can help to improve your aerobic and anaerobic fitness levels. The short rest periods in between the intervals help to keep your heart rate elevated, leading to a greater calorie burn.

HIIT workouts can be done with a variety of exercises, such as running, cycling, jumping jacks, burpees, and many others. They are also adaptable to different fitness levels, as you can adjust the intensity and duration of each interval based on your fitness level.

Overall, HIIT is an effective and efficient way to improve your fitness levels, burn calories, and achieve your fitness goals in a shorter amount of time than other forms of exercise.

Download the PDF here: https://tinyurl.com/HIITExercisebonus

BIOGRAPHY

Ronald J. White has over 30 years of experience as a wellness coach and nutritional consultant, with a primary goal of helping individuals achieve their health objectives. Thanks to his extensive knowledge of nutrition, he has successfully guided many people toward making positive lifestyle changes. Ronald takes an innovative approach to food, which has enabled him to assist countless individuals in reducing inflammation and improving their overall wellbeing. His mission is to empower people to take control of their health and wellbeing by providing them with the tools and knowledge they need to make sustainable lifestyle changes.

The recipes in this book were conceived and written with the invaluable support of his wife Petra, who works as a chef in several restaurants.

If you enjoyed this book, please consider leaving a review on Amazon.
Thank you!

Printed in Great Britain
by Amazon